Praise for Aaron Shepard's
The Business of Writing for Children

BRAVO! I thought it had pretty much all been said, but I was wrong. All the nuts and bolts are here as well as rules that bear repeating, PLUS insights not usually found in how-to books. Clearly and concisely written, this is an invaluable resource for both beginning and more accomplished writers.

**Susan Pearson, Editor-in-Chief,
Lothrop, Lee & Shepard Books**

One of the most comprehensive guides available to anyone wishing to enter the competitive field of children's books. It's all here, from initial idea to successful sale, and then beyond to the essentials of contracts, promotion, and the ABCs of building a successful career. If you're starting out, start out here.

Stephen Mooser, children's author

Here's clearly-written, no-nonsense help for children's writers by a craftsman. Every fledgling author should own this book.

**Stephen Fraser, Executive Editor,
Aladdin Paperbacks**

A wonderful resource. Aaron's experience-based insights into the art and business of children's writing will save beginning writers years of wasted effort—and help published writers achieve long-term success.

Kathleen Duey, children's author

A one-stop shopping center, a complete how-to-do-it guide for the writer who wants a jump-start on looking professional even though he/she may be turning out a first book. Editors will love you if you do it Shepard's way.

Audrey Baird, Editor, *Once Upon A Time*

A clear, concise, straight-ahead starting place for a new writer or a newly-published writer. Shepard knows his stuff!

Jane Yolen, children's author and editor

Covers all the basics of writing for children in a realistic, practical manner. The fun—as well as the work—of writing, selling, and marketing books for young readers is evident in every step of Shepard's approach.

Judith O'Malley, Editor, *Book Links*

A tool every writer needs.

Carol Farley, children's author

This is a book that I would like to gently place into the hands of every aspiring children's book writer. It answers the questions they most often ask, and the questions they really ought to ask. It is realistic without being discouraging, and practical without being cynical.

David K. Brown, librarian and Webmaster,
Children's Literature Web Guide

I carry around a file folder of materials that I share with unpublished writers and illustrators. This book is so comprehensive, I plan to replace my file folder with it. Whether you are a novice or a professional, *The Business of Writing for Children* needs to be in your library. DON'T write a book without it!

Leslie Tryon, children's author/illustrator

A valuable resource!

Barbara Kouts, agent

A generous book—not so much a primer for the would-be writer as an attempt to pass on everything Aaron has learned about writing for children. Full of useful information and tips, it's also a personal and personable account of the joys of scholarship, the fostering of genuine relationships with people like me (editors, publishers, publicists), the love of story.

Jonathan Shaw, Editor,
School Magazine **(Australia)**

Provides both helpful advice and welcome reassurance to authors trying to navigate the complexities of the children's book industry. It is the next best thing to having an experienced author friend in the business.

Susan Salzman Raab, author,
An Author's Guide to Children's Book Promotion,
and children's book publicist, Raab Associates

A clear, concise guide to the often misunderstood field of children's books. No matter what your level of experience—from beginner to veteran—there is much to learn from Aaron Shepard's nuts-and-bolts approach to surviving the bunny-eat-bunny world of writing for children. Read it and learn!

Larry Dane Brimner, children's author

Writers attempting to break into the children's book market will thank Aaron Shepard for graciously sharing his own hard-earned knowledge. I am adding this to my list of must-reads for newcomers to the field.

**Margaret Read MacDonald,
author and librarian**

Aaron's book is worth the price just for the wealth of inside information found in the introduction. For the beginner who wants an in-depth overview of the field, or a pro who needs a shot in the arm, this is an excellent choice.

Dian Curtis Regan, children's author

Finally, a thorough, concise overview of the business end of writing for the children's market. This book is a wonderful gift to the budding authors of the world. Aaron has combined great talents for writing and storytelling with smart and informed business practices to create a great career. Now he shares what he has learned, to help others do the same.

**Kip Nead, co-owner,
Seeds of Change Children's Bookstore**

For aspiring writers of picture book fiction and folktales, this is a great introduction to the complicated world of children's book publishing.

**Harold Underdown,
Senior Editor, Charlesbridge Publishing,
and Webmaster, The Purple Crayon**

A clear, concise, resourceful, often eye-opening guide that is filled with solid advice to help aspiring writers sell their manuscripts and to help published authors boost sales. I learned a good deal from this handy resource. I am sure anyone who is serious about the business of writing for children will profit from it.

Robert D. San Souci, children's author

Also by Aaron Shepard

Picture Books

The Sea King's Daughter: A Russian Legend
The Baker's Dozen: A Saint Nicholas Tale
The Magic Brocade: A Tale of China
Forty Fortunes: A Tale of Iran
The Crystal Heart: A Vietnamese Legend
Master Maid: A Tale of Norway
The Maiden of Northland: A Hero Tale of Finland
The Gifts of Wali Dad: A Tale of India and Pakistan
The Enchanted Storks: A Tale of Bagdad
The Legend of Slappy Hooper: An American Tall Tale
The Legend of Lightning Larry
Savitri: A Tale of Ancient India
Master Man: A Tall Tale of Nigeria (forthcoming)
Lady White Snake: A Tale From Chinese Opera (forthcoming)
Quackling (forthcoming)
The King o' the Cats (forthcoming)
Two-Eyes (forthcoming)
The Princess Mouse: A Tale of Finland (forthcoming)
The Hidden One: A Native American Cinderella Tale
(forthcoming)

Professional Resources

Stories on Stage: Scripts for Reader's Theater

The Business of Writing for Children

An Award-Winning Author's Tips on How to Write, Sell, and Promote Your Children's Books

By Aaron Shepard

Shepard Publications
Los Angeles

Author Online!

For updates and more resources, visit
Aaron Shepard's Kidwriter Page at

www.aaronshep.com/kidwriter

Cover sketch by Toni Goffe, coloring by Angelo Lopez

ISBN 0-938497-11-1

Library of Congress Card Number 99-69759
Library of Congress subject heading:
Children's literature—Authorship

Ordering: Print-on-demand distributors of this book include
Lightning Source (Ingram Book Company), Replica Books
(Baker & Taylor), and Sprout, Inc. It can be ordered through
most U.S. booksellers, both wholesale and retail—but not
from the publisher!

1.1/Lightning

In our time, when the literature for adults is deteriorating, good books for children are the only hope, the only refuge.

Isaac Bashevis Singer

"Thou shalt not" is soon forgotten, but "Once upon a time" lasts forever.

Philip Pullman

A person is a fool to become a writer.

Roald Dahl

Contents

APPENDIX—Resources

About This Book

Let me begin with a word of caution. If you're thinking of taking up children's writing as a lark or as an easy way to make money, my advice is: *Forget it.*

True, there are always those beginning writers who will whip out a children's story, sell it to a publisher on the first try, and wind up with a successful book. But for most of us, entering the profession takes years of practice, self-education, and not a little frustration. And there's more of that *after* we're published.

But if you're serious about writing for children, this book should significantly speed and simplify your professional development. Though not at all meant to be comprehensive, it lays out the basics, points you toward additional resources, and most importantly, provides tips and strategies not commonly found elsewhere. Along with that, it offers detailed looks at some of my own specialties and provides notice of new publishing technologies.

The material comes from several sources. Most of the Introduction, Part 1, and the Appendix is based on handouts created for my former classes and workshops on writing for children. Part 2 consists of articles first written for the *SCBWI Bulletin* and *Once Upon A Time.* All materials have been updated as needed.

Reflecting my own expertise, the focus here is on writing picture book stories and selling them to major publishers. Much of the information, though, will apply to other areas of children's writing as well.

I hope this guide will help in your professional and/or personal growth. Good luck, and don't forget to have fun!

> **Please note: Though comments on this book are welcome, Aaron regrets he cannot provide help individually to aspiring writers.**

Introduction

Dangerous Myths and
Terrible Truths

MYTH: Children's books are easier to write than adult books.

TRUTH: Good writing is difficult no matter what the reader's age—and children deserve the best.

MYTH: Picture books are the easiest children's books to write.

TRUTH: Picture books may be the *hardest*—because they demand conciseness, simplicity, and a visual sense. Also, the competition is greater, because more people try them.

MYTH: A children's book writer must first write for magazines.

TRUTH: Writing for magazines can teach you a lot, but it is different in some ways from book writing. And though magazine credits may catch a book editor's eye, they won't sell your manuscript. If books are your goal, you might do well to jump right in.

MYTH: Children's stories should teach lessons.

TRUTH: Good children's stories do not preach. Instead, they educate for life, by exploring significant themes—as do good adult stories.

MYTH: Since my kids/neighbors/students like my story, it will make a great book.

TRUTH: Your kids/neighbors/students may like it only because it's *yours,* or because they enjoy your reading. This *does not* impress editors.

MYTH: Writing in rhyme will give my story more appeal.

TRUTH: Stories in rhyme are especially hard to do well, so editors look at them skeptically. In most cases, you should avoid rhyme.

MYTH: I must find an illustrator for my picture book manuscript.

TRUTH: Unless you're an artist yourself, editors will want to match you with professional illustrators of their own choice. Sending someone else's pictures with your words can count against you.

MYTH: To sell my work, I must get an agent.

TRUTH: Though it has become harder to sell children's books without an agent, you can still do it—and getting an agent may be as hard as getting a publisher. Agents are more useful and available once you've sold on your own.

MYTH: My chances are better if I submit to small publishers.

TRUTH: Not unless your book is specialized. Small publishers issue fewer books and must often be cautious in their selections. Large publishers can afford to take an occasional chance.

MYTH: Book editors don't like multiple submissions.

TRUTH: Regardless of official pronouncements, most editors no longer discriminate. They sympathize with the reasons for multiple submitting and have even come to expect it.

MYTH: When submitting, I must protect my ideas from theft.

TRUTH: Theft by children's publishers is rare. Ideas are plentiful, so editors are more interested in finding writers who can *handle* ideas. In any case, copyright law protects your work—without any official registration or notice.

MYTH: The longer a publisher takes to answer, the more interested they are in my manuscript.

TRUTH: Your submission could as easily be lost or sitting in a pile unread. Some publishers can take half a year or more to merely glance at your story—or more than a year to politely reject it.

MYTH: Once I've sold my first book, the same publisher will buy more.

TRUTH: Maybe, maybe not. Picture book texts especially are likely to be judged individually, unless you are wildly successful.

MYTH: Once I've sold a book, my writing will support me.

TRUTH: Few published writers are supported entirely by their writing. Most work in regular jobs and write in their spare time. Others supplement their writing with public appearances and teaching.

MYTH: If I write well, I am sure to succeed.

TRUTH: Good writing must be coupled with aggressive, persistent marketing. Otherwise, you might never find an editor who cares enough about your work to publish it—or an audience that cares enough to read it.

PART 1

The Basics

Writing Your Story

Here are the elements that editors, reviewers, and to some extent readers will look for in your story. Take them as general guidelines. Good writers often break rules—but they know when they're doing it!

Theme

A theme is an insight or viewpoint or concept that a story conveys. If an editor says your story is "slight," this may mean you have no significant theme.

Don't blurt out your theme. Let it emerge from the story. If you must come out and say it, do it in dialog, not narration.

Avoid preaching. Children's stories should be explorations of life—not Sunday school lessons.

Keep your theme positive. If writing about a social problem, offer constructive ways for your readers to deal with it.

Plot

Plot is normally built around a conflict involving the main character—for instance, with another character, or with circumstances, or within him- or herself. A story *may* succeed without conflict—especially if for preschoolers—but not without another device to hold attention.

Conflict often takes the form of a problem the main character must resolve. The character should succeed or fail at least in part through his or her own efforts. Most often—especially in realistic fiction—the character learns or grows in the process. *The lesson or growth conveys the theme.*

The conflict should result in increasing dramatic tension, which peaks or "climaxes" towards the end, then resolves.

The basic sequence of plot stages is: arrival of conflict, initial success of the main character, reversals, final victory, and outcome. The success-reversal sequence may repeat.

A novel may have several conflicts, but a short story or picture book should have only one.

Move the plot forward with events and action, rather than with internal musings. *Show, don't tell.*

Story Structure

At the beginning, jump right into the action. At the end, bring the story to a prompt close.

Keep the structure as simple as possible. In a picture book, keep the action in chronological order without "flashbacks" (insertions of earlier scenes).

For a picture book story, make sure you have enough "scenes" (locations) to provide variety in the illustrations. For a magazine story, on the other hand, don't have too many, as space limits the number of scenes that can be illustrated. *The number of scenes determines whether a story is best suited to a picture book or a magazine.*

For your narration, choose as best suits your story between "first person" and "third person." In first person, the story is told by one of its characters—"I did this." In third person, it's told as if by an outside observer—"They did that." First person is popular with middle-grade and young-adult readers as it creates instant intimacy and can convey lively wit and emotion. But it can confuse younger listeners, so it should seldom be used in early picture books. Third person is fine for any age, and permits the writer more sophisticated language and observations.

Whether written in first or third person, the story should generally be told through the eyes of a single character—usually the main character. This is called "point of view." Sudden shifts in the story's point of view can jolt and disorient the reader. To keep it consistent, narrate only what your chosen character would know, and nothing he or she wouldn't—for example, someone else's thought, or something out of sight. If you do need to switch to a different point of view, set up a separate section or chapter for it.

Characters

Before you start writing, know your characters thoroughly.

Your main character should be someone the reader can identify and/or sympathize with. He or she should be near the top age of your intended readers. (One exception is in folktales.)

Identify your characters with one or more telling details—a physical trait, a mannerism, a favorite phrase. A complete description is not needed.

Setting

Set your story in a place and time that will be interesting or familiar.

Style and Tone

Write simply and directly, in short words, short sentences, short paragraphs.

Use dialog wherever possible. Use direct quotes instead of indirect. (Example: "Go away!" instead of "He told her to go away.") Aim to make dialog at least one-third of your story.

Avoid big chunks of narration—especially description. Often you can split it into smaller pieces, or convey information in dialog. (Example: "I like your purple hair.")

Use language that creates an atmosphere or "tone" suited to your story.

For younger children, use poetic devices like rhythm, repetition, alliteration ("Peter Piper picked a peck"), and rhyme—though generally not in verse.

Avoid being cutesy or sweet or sentimental or condescending.

> The strongest children's stories have well-developed themes, engaging plots, suitable structure, memorable characters, well-chosen settings, and attractive style. For best results, build strength in *all* areas.

WriterSpeak #1: Book Categories

These names and definitions are offered as general guide-lines only. They vary from publisher to publisher, and may be stretched for manuscripts of high quality. Also, please be aware that *books are getting shorter!* The given manuscript lengths are based on manuscript pages of about 250 words.

Picture book. A book in which illustrations balance or dominate the text, most often with large pages. Typically, text and art are mingled on the page. Includes some "plotless" books—alphabet, counting, concept. For preschool to kindergarten. Book length is usually a standard 32 pages, but can be less. Manuscript length is two to four pages.

Picture story book. A picture book with more text and plot development. Typically, text and art are separated on the page, and the text could stand alone. For kindergarten to grade 3 or higher. Book length is still usually 32 pages, but can be more. Manuscript length is five to nine pages. Note: Though the distinction between **picture books** and **picture story books** can be helpful to a writer or illustrator, the two types are most often lumped together as **picture books.**

Board book. A short picture book on stiffened pages. Often "plotless." Most often published in a series. For up to age 2. Manuscript length is one page or less.

> Books in the categories above are meant to be read first *to* children. Books in the categories below are meant to be read mostly *by* children.

Easy reader. An illustrated book for beginning readers, with text dominating pictures. Often split into several stories. For grades 1 and 2. Manuscript length is one to twenty pages. Examples: Dr. Seuss's *The Cat in the Hat*, Arnold Lobel's *Frog and Toad*.

Chapter book. A short, illustrated novel, split into brief chapters. For grades 2 and 3. Manuscript length is forty to sixty pages. Examples: Daniel Pinkwater's *The Hoboken Chicken Emergency*, Stephen Manes's *Be a Perfect Person in Just Three Days!*

Young nonfiction. Nonfiction in picture book format. For grades 2 and 3. Manuscript length is ten to twenty pages.

Middle-grade book. For grades 4 to 6. Manuscript pages: novels—100-150; nonfiction—60-100. Published in a slightly oversized paperback format.

Young adult book. For grades 7 and up, but mostly to grade 9. Manuscript pages: novels—175-200; romance—140-160; nonfiction—100-150. Published in standard paperback format.

The "age" of your manuscript is determined by a combination of page length, chapter length, complexity (of language, structure, plot, etc.), subject matter, theme, and *age of main character*.

Submitting Your Manuscript

Note: Sample manuscript pages follow this section.

Submission Format

Manuscripts must above all be neat and easily readable. Use normal 20-lb. bond paper such as for photocopying. Print on one side only. Do not use colored paper. Do not staple or bind. (A paper clip is OK.)

Use a plain, simple font—nothing fancy or artsy or cute—in a 12- or 14-point size. Double-space your text and set margins all around of at least 1 inch. Full pages should average about 250 words. *Do not* "justify" your text—it should be flush left with a ragged (uneven) right edge.

First manuscript page: At top left, on single-spaced lines below the top margin, place your name, address, phone, fax, email, and Web page. At top right, for a magazine piece, note the word count and the rights being sold—generally either First Serial Rights or Reprint Rights. Though nothing is required at top right for a book manuscript, you can place here a word count and/or brief notices like "Manuscript return not requested." (On your computer, this can all be placed in a first-page-only header, with a two-cell table to set text blocks side by side.)

One-third to halfway down the first page, on double-spaced lines, put your story title, any subtitle, and your "byline"—

your name as you want it to appear on the published work. These lines can be centered or else flush left like the rest of the text. For a picture book, a dedication line can follow. Next, in brackets, give any essential notes to the editor or others—for example, a notice of the story's previous publication. (Brackets set a note apart from the text.)

All other manuscript pages: At top left, on a single line above the top margin and a half inch or so from the top of the page, put your last name, a comma, then a keyword or two from the title. On the same line at top right goes the page number. (On your computer, this can all be placed in a header to appear on every page but the first. Use a right tab for the page number, and automatic page numbering.)

For a picture book or magazine piece, start your story on the first page, below the other text. For a longer work, start a new page for each new element—dedication, table of contents, chapters, and so on.

Do not place a copyright notice on your manuscript. It can mark you as an amateur! Your writing is protected by law without any such notice.

In a cover letter, you can tell the following: your story title, your qualifications (previous publications, work with children, SCBWI membership), intriguing background to the story, why it is being submitted to this editor/publisher, a reminder of previous contact. Be brief and do not retell the story. An author flyer or one-sheet resumé can replace much of this. A Post-it can often replace a cover letter.

If you're not an illustrator yourself, leave all illustration and design to the publisher. *Do not* find an illustrator on your own. Do not send sketches or a "dummy" (mock-up of a book) or show page turns. Do not write notes describing illustrations—unless an essential element *cannot* be described in your text. (If that is the case, enclose the note in brackets.)

Send submissions in a full-size or half-size envelope. If you want the manuscript back, include an SASE (self-addressed stamped envelope) for return. If you don't want it, say so clearly and include just a standard business-size SASE for reply. (For foreign reply-only, it's OK to omit the SASE.)

Do not use gimmicks like perfume, balloons, recordings, etc.

Submit by computer file only if that is requested or specifically allowed. Follow publisher instructions on format and delivery method—email, floppy disk, CD. When in doubt, submit in Microsoft Word format using DOS filename conventions—a maximum of eight letters, then a period and the "doc" extension (as in "story.doc"). The extension is most important for email attachments, as it tells email programs how to handle the file. If you're on a Mac with a floppy disk drive but a PC disk is required, you can convert a Mac disk by specifying the DOS disk format while erasing it.

Before submitting a manuscript, you may want to send a "query"—a letter asking whether an editor is interested. Queries are most useful for nonfiction, less for fiction, and least for picture books. The query can include your qualifications, the manuscript's approach, its intended readership, and how it stands out from the competition. Include an SASE. If an editor has already worked with you, the query may be sent by email. Querying may get you permission to submit to publishers that don't read "unsolicited" manuscripts. It can also be used to offer a choice of manuscripts.

Halfway between a manuscript and a query is a "proposal." Used for longer works only, the proposal includes the same kind of information as in a query, plus an outline/synopsis and one to three sample chapters. A proposal is often submitted when an author wants to sell a book before writing it all—but this works only for authors who have already proven themselves. Proposals can also be sent in place of a manuscript already finished, to help speed initial consideration. In the end, though, this may actually slow things down, as an editor interested by your proposal will likely still want to see everything you have before deciding finally.

Submission Strategies

Don't send out anything before getting it critiqued by professionals or peers.

Research the book markets by reading *current* children's books, studying market guides, and writing to publishers for their catalogs. Research the magazine markets by reading *current* issues, studying market guides, and writing to magazines for writer guidelines.

You can get book editor names from market guides or by calling the publisher. (For best luck, try the marketing department instead of the editorial department.) Addressing your submission to a specific editor raises your chances of a timely and/or personal response. On the other hand, your manuscript might otherwise be routed to a more suitable editor.

For picture books, you might combine two manuscripts in one submission. This saves time and postage, and shows that you are not a single-book writer.

Keep a careful record of each submission. Include publisher, editor addressed (if any), submission date, editor replying (if any), and response.

Publisher bans on "unsolicited" (unrequested) manuscript submissions are often meant only to discourage amateur writers. A professional-level submission addressed to a specific editor will normally get at least a glance—even if the reply denies this! (Note: Bans on unsolicited manuscripts are never applied to submissions from agents. For this reason, many editors themselves confuse the meaning of the term, saying "unsolicited" when they mean "unagented.")

"Multiple submissions"—manuscripts sent to a number of publishers for simultaneous consideration—are now accepted by most book publishers without stigma. For beginning writers, I recommend submitting a manuscript to at least three places at once—and until you are known, these could even be imprints at the same publishing house.

Most publishers ask to be informed when a submission is multiple—but for beginners, informing or not seems to make no real difference, and some editors even advise against it! In the end, it is really up to you. If you do choose to give notice, it can be placed in a cover letter, on a Post-it, or at top right on the first manuscript page. Use a tactful phrase like, "This is one of several circulating copies."

There might well be times when you find it's best to submit a book manuscript for exclusive rather than simultaneous consideration—for instance, if an editor has bought an earlier manuscript. If so, you should set a limit to how long this will last—perhaps three months. Give notice of this limit only when and if you first tell the editor that the submission is exclusive. When the time is up, leave the manuscript with that editor without further notice and send it elsewhere as a multiple submission.

If you have submitted multiply, and one publisher accepts your manuscript, be sure to inform the other publishers promptly.

The comments above on multiple submissions apply to book manuscripts only. Magazine pieces should *never* be submitted multiply except in noncompeting markets—such as for different religious denominations or different countries. However, queries can always be sent multiply.

Even a great story can be rejected for reasons outside your control. But consider carefully whether the problem might be in your manuscript. If so, you can revise and resubmit.

Since most rejections are form letters, a signed, personal rejection note from an editor should be taken as encouragement. You will probably want to submit work to that editor again. But if you don't like what the editor said, you can submit instead to a different editor at that publisher or imprint.

If you get no reply in three or four months, it's OK to write or call to check the status of your manuscript—though this may have little effect on response time. (When writing, it may help to include a self-addressed, stamped postcard.) Remember, editors are no more efficient or responsible than anyone else!

If you are submitting multiply, there is little point in ever withdrawing a manuscript kept too long—though a threat to do so shortly may get it read.

After sending off one manuscript, work on another. Submit often to the same publishers/editors to build recognition and credibility. Think in terms of career, not single works.

In all things, be professional. Writing is art, but marketing is business!

Aaron Shepard
P.O. Box 555
Hometown, CA 55555 USA
555-555-5555
Fax: 555-555-5555
AS@aaronshep.com
www.aaronshep.com

The Legend of Lightning Larry

By Aaron Shepard

For Danny, Cate, and Ishi

Well, you've heard about gunfighting good guys like Wild Bill Hickok and Wyatt Earp. But I'll tell you a name that strikes even greater fear into the hearts of bad men everywhere.

Lightning Larry.

I'll never forget the day Larry rode into our little town of Brimstone and walked into the Cottonmouth Saloon. He strode up to the bar and smiled straight at the bartender.

"Lemonade, please," he said.

Every head in the place turned to look.

Now, standing next to Larry at the bar was Crooked Curt. Curt was one of a band of rustlers and thieves that had been terrorizing our town, led by a ferocious outlaw named Evil-Eye McNeevil.

Curt was wearing the usual outlaw scowl. Larry turned to him and

Picture Book Manuscript—First Page

smiled. "Mighty big frown you got there, mister," he said.

"What's it to you?" growled Curt.

"Well," said Larry, "maybe I could help remove it."

"I'd like to see you try!" said Curt.

The rest of us got out of the way, real fast. The bartender ducked behind the bar. Larry and Curt moved about ten paces from each other, hands at the ready. Larry was still smiling.

Curt moved first. But he only just cleared his gun from its holster before Larry aimed and fired.

Zing!

There was no bang and no bullet. Just a little bolt of light that hit Curt right in the heart.

Curt just stood there, his eyes wide with surprise. Then he dropped his gun, and a huge grin spread over his face. He rushed up to Larry and pumped his hand.

"I'm mighty glad to know you, stranger!" he shouted. "The drinks are on me! Lemonade for everyone!"

When Evil-Eye McNeevil and his outlaw gang heard that Crooked Curt had gone straight, they shuddered right down to their boots.

Most any outlaw would rather die than smile!

Evil-Eye's men were shook up, but they weren't about to let on. The very next day, Dismal Dan, Devilish Dick, and Dreadful Dave rode into Brimstone, yelling like crazy men and shooting wild. Windows shattered and citizens scattered.

Then Lightning Larry showed up. He never warned them. Never even stopped smiling. Just shot three little bolts of light. Hit those outlaws right in the heart.

Picture Book Manuscript—Second Page

WriterSpeak #2: Book Publishers

Trade publisher. Generally publishes books in hardcover and/or quality paperback, and possibly also in ebook, audiobook, and other formats. Sells directly and indirectly to bookstores, libraries, and schools. Typically offers royalties and an advance. Trade books are the most likely to be reviewed in important publications and to be purchased widely by bookstores and libraries. Most large trade publishers are in New York City. Often called publishing "houses," many of them shelter various "imprints"— publishing divisions under independent editorial direction.

Small press or **small publisher** or **independent publisher.** A trade publisher much smaller than the giants in New York. May sell through the same channels as large publishers and/or depend mostly on mail order sales. May offer royalties with medium to no advance, or a flat fee. Books are often specialized in subject and/or approach. NOTE: Few small presses can match the editorial, design, promotion, or distribution capabilities of a large publisher. Still, a small press might put more care into your book and keep it in print longer, and might also market smarter to a specialized audience. And as mergers and acquisitions thin the ranks of the giants and make them less hospitable to new writers, smaller presses are bound to evolve to take up the slack.

ePublisher. A small press that publishes ebooks (electronic books) in one or more formats, and possibly also "hardcopy" books through print-on-demand. An epublisher typically offers an extremely high royalty with no advance. Because of low production costs and the large number of startups, finding an epublisher for your book can be much easier than finding another kind. Sales and prestige, though, are most often correspondingly lower. Some epublishers are actually subsidy publishers (see below).

Mass market publisher. Publishes mostly small-format paperbacks. Sells directly and indirectly to bookstores and other retail outlets—discount stores, supermarkets, etc. Typically offers royalties and an advance. The books are not often reviewed, but can achieve impressive distribution.

Educational publisher. Publishes educational materials for sale through specialized channels. May offer royalties with minimal or no advance, or a flat fee.

Religious publisher. Publishes religious materials for sale through specialized channels. May offer royalties with minimal or no advance, or a flat fee.

Book packager or developer. Sells ideas for single books or series to publishers, then subcontracts with writers and illustrators for content. May offer royalties with minimal or no advance, or a flat fee. Can provide steady work, but often with low pay and no recognition.

Subsidy or co-op or vanity publisher. Publishes books for a fee. NOTE: Regardless of claims, subsidy publishers do not effectively promote or distribute books. Traditionally, writers have been advised to avoid them, as the product is much the same as from self-publishing but at a much higher price. Today, though, new subsidy publishers using print-on-demand and/or ebook technology may in effect offer self-publishing at a reasonable cost.

Negotiating Your Contract

The Initial Offer

When an editor accepts your book manuscript, she will make an initial offer. This usually includes a royalty and an advance.

Royalty. This is a percentage to be paid to you for each copy sold. Larger publishers usually make it a percentage of "list"—the price listed on the cover. Smaller and specialty publishers often base it instead on "net"—the amount paid to the publisher after discounts—or may just offer a flat fee. Though "list" is much more than "net," large publishers have a way of reducing your royalties in a variety of circumstances, so the final difference in what you make might not be that great.

Typical royalties are 10% for hardcover and 6% for softcover. For picture books, these percentages will be divided between writer and illustrator. Ask for those standard rates if your editor offers less, but don't ask to exceed them.

ePublishers—specialty publishers of ebooks—often give a *much* higher royalty, though most often on very low sales.

Advance. This is money paid to you before and/or on publication and charged against your future royalties and other income from the book. Typical first-time advances are $1,000 to $5,000, though smaller publishers may offer none at all.

You can almost always get an initial offer for the advance raised $500 to $1000, because editors usually start low to allow for this. It is important that you request it, for several reasons. First, it shows you are a professional. Second, the more paid for the book, the more likely that it will be valued and promoted. Third, THE ADVANCE IS THE ONLY INCOME YOU CAN COUNT ON FROM THE BOOK.

You will commonly be asked to accept payment of the advance in up to three installments: one on signing the contract, one on submitting an "acceptable" final manuscript (after basic editing and revision), and one on publication. Try to reduce this to one early payment, or at most, two. Making you wait until publication is usually only a way to delay paying what is due to you. For a picture book, it could mean your waiting many years—or not being paid at all, if your editor leaves and the book is canceled. Also questionable may be the publisher requiring an "acceptable" final manuscript before a second installment, since often only minor editing is needed—but this might not be negotiable.

Your First Contract

When the advance and royalty have been agreed on, the editor will send you a contract. For your first one, watch for the following:

Subsidiary rights. Your publisher will offer for sale to other publishers the rights to issue your work in various forms and editions. Income from the most important rights is split 50%-50% between publisher and author (and split again evenly between a picture book's author and its illustrator). Other splits may be more in your favor, and you can ask for this if they're not. Recommended:

First serial (for periodicals)—80%-20%
Foreign editions, in English—75%-25%
Foreign editions, in translation—65%-35%
Mechanical/electronic/recording—75%-25%
Commercial/merchandising—75%-25%
Dramatic/movie/radio—75%-25%

Though an agent would entirely reserve some of these rights to sell for you, you're not usually in a position to sell them on your own—so it's unwise to try to reserve any unless you know a likely buyer. On the other hand, you might ask for reversion of any rights the publisher has not sold or exercised within a certain period—say, two years after publication.

Option. This clause gives the publisher the right to buy your next book. This is fair, but make sure there's a limit of two to three months for the publisher to decide. You should also have the right to decline the offer if you don't like the terms. Finally, you might request automatic voiding of the option if your editor leaves.

Publication. Make sure there is a clause committing the publisher to issue the book within a certain time—typically eighteen months from receipt of the finished manuscript, or of the finished art in the case of a picture book.

Reserve against returns. Publishers temporarily withhold a percentage of royalties to allow for books returned unsold by booksellers. Since returns are seldom great after the first two years, you might try to limit this practice to that period.

Wraparound. If your book does not sell enough copies to "earn out" the advance, a wraparound clause will make you pay it off with income from any past or future books with that publisher. If the contract has such a clause, get it deleted or don't sign!

Reversion of rights. Make sure the contract enables you to regain rights to the book if it goes out of print. Make sure too that the contract's definition of "in print" says that foreign editions don't count. (Note: Authors are sometimes advised to ask also for automatic reversion of rights in the event of publisher bankruptcy. But ownership after bankruptcy is governed entirely by a legal trustee, so such contract clauses are not valid or useful.)

Author's copies. You can usually get 15 free copies of a hardcover edition or 25 copies of a paperback. Also make sure you can purchase extra copies at 40% to 50% off.

Note: At this writing, new technologies of electronic publishing and print-on-demand have engendered a battle between authors and agents on one hand and publishers on the other. A number of issues have arisen, such as the proper split of income from ebook editions and whether future books are ever to be considered out of print. It is too early to offer definitive advice in this area, so keep an eye on discussions in writer publications and elsewhere. Be aware, though, that for most books, the money in question will not amount to much.

Future Contracts

Your negotiating position with a particular publisher improves with each new contract. After your first, watch for the following:

Advance. This should go up automatically each time.

Royalty. If your first royalty was low, you can probably raise it to standard level for your second book.

Escalation. If you don't have one, ask for an "escalation clause" to raise your royalty after a certain number of copies are sold. A typical escalation for hardcover might give 12% after sales of 15,000 to 20,000 copies. For paperback, an escalation might be to 8% after 25,000 to 50,000 copies.

General Hints

When an editor offers a contract, it means she very much wants your book and has already invested considerable time in the acceptance process. Don't be afraid to ask questions or request changes! You may not get what you want—but as long as you stay reasonable, you won't jeopardize the sale.

A publisher's contract can be confusing and intimidating, but it is in English and can be understood with a little study and patience. If you simply can't deal with it, you might find an agent to handle it for a 10% to 15% commission or a flat fee. Your editor might recommend one. For a fee, you could also hire a lawyer to negotiate the contract—but be sure to find one who specializes in "intellectual property."

Many new authors agonize over clauses that can't be changed and that usually make no difference. While it's true that contracts tend to be stacked in favor of the publisher, that's just the nature of the business. And keep in mind that few first books ever earn more than their advance anyway. So, relax and enjoy the check!

The Publishing Process

From Manuscript to Book

Editing. Your editor will send you a copy of your manuscript marked with requested changes and suggestions for revision. If your editor does her job well, this can be a great benefit to you and your book. But if there are things you can't accept, inform your editor respectfully and give reasons. In most cases, your wishes will be honored.

Copyediting. After you've revised the manuscript, it will be copyedited—most often by a different editor—focusing on details like spelling, grammar, word usage, and punctuation. The marked manuscript will be sent to you for review and approval. THIS IS YOUR LAST GOOD CHANCE TO MAKE CHANGES IN YOUR WRITING.

Design. The art director or another book designer will decide on book size, type size and style, paper, cover materials, and so on.

Typesetting. From a computer file supplied by you or created by the publisher, your manuscript will be formatted in the type chosen for the book. You will be sent a copy of the "galleys" to check for errors. At this point, you can still make minor changes—but don't start rewriting! If your book is not a picture book, this step may be skipped in favor of sending "page proofs" (see below).

Illustrating. If your book is to be illustrated, the edited manuscript or the galleys will be sent to the artist, who is chosen by the editor, often with help from the art director. In most cases, you have little or no say on the art, even if you are shown samples as a courtesy. In general, this makes good sense, since most authors think they know more about art than they do. Picture book writers must keep in mind that the artist is a creative *collaborator*, not a mere translator of the author's words. Still, you might ask to check the artist's preliminary sketches for consistency with your text.

Layout. The type and any illustrations are arranged in page form with a computer publishing program. You may receive "page proofs" for checking, and certainly you will if there were no galleys.

Printing and binding. Most book printing presses use metal printing plates, which are produced by the printer from the publisher's computer files. Full-color books require separate plates for each of three colors plus black, for printing over the same sheet to produce specific shades. Newer presses may print directly from computer files, without plates. The book is printed on both sides of large sheets, generally with 16 to 32 pages on each sheet, front and back. For hardcover, these "signatures" are folded, sewn, trimmed, and glued into a cover. For paperback, they are folded, glued into a cover, and trimmed.

Electronic publishing. The publisher's computer files might also be converted to one or more special electronic formats for sale as ebooks. This is most likely for books with few or no illustrations. In some cases, a publisher might skip the print edition entirely and go directly to ebook.

Print-on-demand. Books that sell out their regular printings but do not have sales justifying reprint may continue to be made available through print-on-demand. With this technology, books are printed one at a time, as ordered. The machines used are laser printers, related to the ones you might buy for your home office but much faster and more sophisticated. In some cases, a publisher might skip traditional printing and go directly to print-on-demand. At this writing, the technology is limited to black and white for text pages, so it cannot be used for picture books—but this may change.

From Book to Reader

Publication date. The marketing of your book revolves around this date, which is the month your book is "officially" published. It normally falls at least a month after the book is actually available, so copies can be sent ahead to reviewers and bookstores. Publication dates are grouped mostly into two "seasons," spring and fall—though some large publishers add winter and/or summer. The publisher's books for each season are called the publisher's "list," and are generally featured in a seasonal catalog.

Publicity. Long before publication, the publicity department will ask you for information about yourself and your book, and for a personal photo. It's important that you supply these! They will be used in preparing and sending publicity materials, and probably also on the book itself. (But some information, such as mailing lists, may be better sent closer to the publication date.) When your book is ready, typically several hundred review copies will be sent out. But the reviews—or lack of them—from just a few big library and trade journals will most affect the book's chances of success.

Sales. Months before your book's season, your editor will present the book (or whatever is ready of it) at a national conference for the publisher's sales force. The salespeople, or "publisher reps," will then visit or phone the stores and other accounts in their "territories," presenting books on the publisher's list and taking orders. (Smaller publishers may sell through independent, contracted sales forces, through one or more distributors, and/or through mail order.) The reps will focus on books they judge most likely to sell—so they have great power over what shows up in stores!

Advertising. In most cases, advertising does not sell children's books. So your first book will probably not be advertised, except in general ads for the season's list.

Promotion. Promoting new authors seldom pays off in the short run, so the promotion department saves its major efforts and dollars for authors already prominent. It will usually help you with arrangements for individual events like school visits and local bookstore signings, but you may find it simpler to handle these on your own. Still, keeping the department informed of what you do can sometimes inspire matching efforts. And if you stick with the publisher, your turn may come for big-time promotion.

WriterSpeak #3: Booksellers

Wholesaler. Buys books in quantity from publishers and distributors at a deep discount, then sells to retailers, libraries, and sometimes schools. With local or regional warehousing and a broad range of titles, wholesalers serve as convenient middlemen. Typically, a bookstore might order a new book first from the publisher or distributor, then rely on a wholesaler for quick restocking. Two giants dominate this field: Ingram and Baker & Taylor. Traditionally, Ingram has sold mostly to retailers, and B&T has sold mostly to libraries, but the two have been gradually encroaching on each other's territories.

Distributor. Buys the books of a number of publishers at a very deep discount—either by outright purchase or on consignment—and sells to wholesalers, retailers, and sometimes libraries and schools. The distributor's sales of a publisher's books might be exclusive in certain markets, in certain regions, or for the entire book trade. Unlike a wholesaler, which merely waits for orders to arrive, a distributor has active salespeople. (Some distributors, though, may act as wholesalers with books they don't distribute.) Publishers who sell through distributors are generally smaller ones without their own sales forces. One prominent distributor is Publishers Group West.

Retailer. Buys books from publishers, distributors, and/or wholesalers at a discount, then sells to the final purchaser. Retailers take many forms, including bookstore, online bookseller, book club, book fair, mass merchandiser, and warehouse club.

Bookstore. The largest of the bookstore retailers are super-store chains like Barnes & Noble and Borders, and these will generally sell the most copies of a book. But independent (locally-owned) children's bookstores are also influential and sometimes determine a book's fate. These stores are usually owned and staffed by people who know and care deeply about children's books. Though few authors can afford to take sides in the battle between chains and independents, you will find the smaller stores worthy of your support.

Online bookseller. With virtually no limits to the breadth and depth of their catalogs and no need to stock all books they sell, online booksellers provide a unique chance for slower-selling books to remain in public reach. They're also the most natural and convenient outlets for ebooks. Online bookselling is dominated by Amazon.com, followed by on-line branches of superstore chains, like BarnesandNoble.com and Borders.com. All three of these enable authors to submit corrections and supplementary materials for their catalogs. All three also offer affiliate programs by which an author can earn a commission from book sales made through links from his or her Web site. The small amount of money nor-mally earned, though, may not be worth the possible price of showing favoritism among booksellers.

Book club. A children's book club can sell either to parents, or to students with the help of teachers. The three biggest school book clubs are Scholastic, Trumpet, and Troll. The biggest for parents is Children's Book-of-the-Month Club. A club may print its own cheap paperback edition of a book, and so act as publisher as well. Though books sold by a club bring in a lower royalty per book, the high sales volume can mean significant earnings and exposure and even help sales of the regular edition. Usually, a book is submitted to clubs by its publisher—but authors can submit their own.

Book fair. A book fair company sells books through portable book displays. Typically, a children's book fair is hosted and run by a school, which is given a percentage of sales. Book fair companies use the publisher's standard edition instead of printing their own. This field is dominated by Scholastic, and its selection of a book can mean extensive exposure. Like book clubs, book fair companies will consider a book that is submitted by the author—but for book fairs, it must already be in paperback.

Mass merchandisers and warehouse clubs. Outlets like Wal-Mart, Sam's Club, and Costco buy in quantity from the publisher at extremely deep discounts and likewise heavily discount their sales. Books sold this way bring a much-reduced royalty to the author. In most cases, though, the book is bought by someone who would otherwise never come across it—so authors should generally welcome the added income and exposure.

Building Your Career

Starting Out

Keep writing! Like any other skill, writing takes practice. You learn as you go.

Spend time with kids.

Read lots of current books in the genre and age group you're writing for.

Read magazines and newsletters—for writers, publishers, booksellers, librarians, educators, anyone involved with children's books.

Take classes with qualified children's writers.

Join a critique group, or exchange manuscripts with other writers. Detailed feedback is *essential* for most new writers, and you're not likely to get it at first from editors.

Attend conferences and conventions. You will not only learn but will make valuable personal contacts.

Join the Society of Children's Book Writers and Illustrators!

Upon Publication

Keep doing all the above.

Develop a good relationship with your editor and other publishing personnel. Be professional and cooperative. Keep in close touch with them, and let them know what you're doing. Make them eager to publish and promote you more.

Make friends with your local media. A newspaper is the most likely to be interested in your work, perhaps printing a feature story as well as reviewing your books. The smaller the town where you live, the better your chances for media attention.

Make frequent public appearances. This both promotes your books and supports your writing—in fact, the fees can double your author's income! Contact educators, librarians, bookstore managers, and event planners, to tell them you're available. Here are some possibilities:

- Visit schools.
- Read for a library story hour.
- Autograph books at a bookstore.
- Speak at a conference.
- Teach a class at a college.

Create a Web page to help people find you and your books. Feature free resources for education and/or entertainment—resources that potential book buyers will seek out. Register your own domain name to gain a simple and permanent Web address for your page and a permanent email address for yourself. Then make sure the Web address is included in all information about you.

Long Term

Keep doing all the above.

Think in terms of career. Publication of your first book is only the first of many steps in building a career as a children's author.

Being a children's author is more than just writing. Your books will sell best when you sell yourself. Plan to spend maybe a third of your "writing" time on appearances, correspondence, Web site maintenance, and other forms of promotion.

Try to keep in the public eye by publishing at least one book a year. It takes about eight to ten books to "establish" a children's author!

Select your writing projects carefully. The focus and direction of your work as a whole will help or hinder your career.

Consider writing for different age groups. The more age groups you cover, the more chances you'll get to promote your work.

Consider writing sequels. If one of your books is popular, readers will want to read more about those characters. A sequel or two can have a multiplier effect on popularity.

The more books you have with a single publisher, the more the publisher may want to promote you. Still, if you write more than one book a year, or if your publisher does not want all your work, consider trying for more than one publisher. Publishers are seldom as loyal to authors as they once were, and editors are more likely than ever to change or lose their jobs—so having more than one publisher can provide a margin of safety. And a little competition among publishers seldom hurts an author.

Agents are seldom available to beginning writers, and may or may not do better than you could yourself. Besides, through your own marketing efforts you gain valuable knowledge of your field. But at some point you might want to acquire an agent to share your work load, give you access to new editors, and/or maximize your earnings. If so, choose carefully! As in every other field, there are good and bad, and a bad agent can ruin your career. Also be aware that *no* agent can give your career as much time and attention as you can yourself. And agents—like publishers—must focus their efforts on their most profitable authors. So, take care not to hound your agent, but do check on progress, now and then.

Most important of all is to write great books. "Publishable" isn't good enough—aim to write classics!

PART 2

The Inside Story

Script Your Story!

Note: Sample reader's theater script pages follow this article.

Manuscripts from beginning writers often bog down from lack of enough dialog and action. If you have this problem, here's a suggestion: Script your story!

Since I have no kids, my introduction to children's literature was somewhat unusual. In 1986, I was in need of a part-time job and, being already interested in storytelling—for adults—I arranged to join a reader's theater troupe. This wonderful organization had been professionally performing adaptations of children's literature in public schools throughout the county for over a decade. I soon discovered that I loved performing for kids, and loved children's literature as well.

My five years with the troupe taught me to think of stories *primarily* in terms of dialog and action—because these are the main components of performance. (Though reader's theater is often performed without stage movement, the group that I worked with would mime the stories to help keep young people's interest.) I learned that kids are almost entirely focused on what characters do and say. In fact, they watch the characters even while a narrator is speaking.

After awhile, I began contributing my own adaptations of favorite stories to the troupe's repertoire, and this led to other discoveries. I found that some stories required drastic

---

From the *SCBWI Bulletin,* February-March 1994.

simplification and cuts in narration to make them work in performance.

On the other hand, stories from some of the best and most popular children's authors almost scripted themselves. Nearly all that was needed was to take out the "tags"—the "he saids" and "she saids"—and split the text into character and narrator speaking parts. These authors were already writing to create vivid, living scenes on the stage of the child's imagination—the reader's theater of the mind.

Today, when I write my own stories, one corner of my mind is always asking, "How does this work on stage?" As a result, I turn out stories that are—I hope—lively and interesting to kids.

Not every children's writer can have the benefit of years in reader's theater. But any children's writer can use reader's theater techniques to test or enhance their writing. Here's how:

Try sitting down with one of your short story or picture book manuscripts and adapting it into a script. Just split up the text into speaking parts for characters and a narrator, adding an identifier in front of each speech. Leave out tags that don't contain important information.

What happens? Do the characters have enough to say? Or are they waiting around for the narrator to get through a page or two? As a rule of thumb, most narrator speeches should consist of only one or two kid-sized paragraphs. (Allow an extra paragraph where there's a "scene change.") No more than two or three narrator speeches should be any longer.

If that's not what you have, check whether you need all that narration, or whether you can move some of the character dialog into the middle, or—best yet—whether you can convert narration into speeches for the characters. *A narrator should say only what the characters can't.*

While you're there, check your action. Visualize the stage and how the characters are going to move on it. Does it all make sense? Did you describe something physically impossible? Did you leave out something vital? Is it too busy? Not busy enough? Is the number of characters about right, or is the stage too crowded?

If you're brave, you could test the script by asking critique group members or other friends to read it while you listen. And if you're positively courageous, you and your friends could perform it for kids!

Another useful approach would be to write a story *first* as a script. This would practically guarantee enough dialog and action. Afterwards, you could join together the text and insert the tags.

A good script can have other uses too. At least one top children's magazine has been looking—with little success—for short scripts to complement its stories. Scripts can also be used in promotion. For instance, when you start visiting schools, classes might like to perform scripts of your publications.

So consider scripting your stories. It can give you valuable insights into your work, provide new avenues of publication and promotion, and be great fun as well.

Savitri
A Tale of Ancient India

Retold by Aaron Shepard

Adapted for reader's theater by the author, from the picture book
published by Whitman, Morton Grove, Illinois, 1992

| Aaron Shepard | AS@aaronshep.com | www.aaronshep.com |

GENRE: Myth   READING LEVEL: Grades 4-9
CULTURE: India (ancient)   READERS: 10
THEME: Strength of will   TIME: 10 min.

ROLES: Narrator 1, Narrator 2, Savitri, Satyavan, King 1, King 2, Teacher,
Narada, Yama, Goddess

NOTE: This story is probably around 3000 years old. It was first written down
about 2000 years ago as part of the *Mahabharata*, India's great national epic.
Savitri is pronounced "SAH-vit-ree." *Satyavan* is pronounced "SOT-yuh-von."
Narada is pronounced "NAH-ruh-duh." *Yama* is pronounced "YAH-muh."
Mahabharata is pronounced "MAH-hah-BAH-ruh-tuh."

NARRATOR 1: In India, in the time of legend, there lived a king
with many wives but not one child. Morning and evening for
eighteen years, he faced the fire on the sacred altar and prayed for the
gift of children.

NARRATOR 2: Finally, a shining goddess rose from the flames.

GODDESS: I am Savitri, child of the Sun. By your prayers, you have
won a daughter.

Reader's Theater Script—First Page

NARRATOR 1: Within a year, a daughter came to the king and his favorite wife. He named her Savitri, after the goddess.

NARRATOR 2: Beauty and intelligence were the princess Savitri's, and eyes that shone like the sun. So splendid was she, people thought she herself was a goddess. Yet when the time came for her to marry, no man asked for her. Her father told her,

KING 1: Weak men turn away from radiance like yours. Go out and find a man worthy of you. Then I will arrange the marriage.

NARRATOR 1: In the company of servants and councilors, Savitri traveled from place to place. After many days, she came upon a hermitage by a river crossing. Here lived many who had left the towns and cities for a life of prayer and study.

NARRATOR 2: Savitri entered the hall of worship and bowed to the eldest teacher. As they spoke, a young man with shining eyes came into the hall. He guided another man, old and blind.

SAVITRI: *(softly, to the teacher)* Who is that young man?

TEACHER: *(smiling)* That is Prince Satyavan. He guides his father, a king whose realm was conquered. It is well that Satyavan's name means "Son of Truth," for no man is richer in virtue.

NARRATOR 1: When Savitri returned home, she found her father with the holy seer called Narada.

KING 1: Daughter, have you found a man you wish to marry?

SAVITRI: Yes, father. His name is Satyavan.

NARADA: *(gasps)* Not Satyavan! Princess, no man could be more worthy, but you must not marry him! I know the future. Satyavan will die, one year from today!

Reader's Theater Script—Second Page

Words That Make Pictures

When I speak at a school, library, or bookstore, I usually read one of my works in progress. Afterwards, I might ask one of the adults, "Do you think that story would make a good picture book?"

"Oh, yes!" is the frequent answer. "I could see all the pictures!"

That's what I aim for. In the words of a long-forgotten source, "I write words that make pictures."

I'm not talking about colorful metaphors or spicy adjectives or loads of descriptive detail. I'm talking about drawing readers into the story and engaging their imaginations, so they create the pictures themselves.

To draw readers in, you must be concrete. To keep them there, you must be invisible.

Being Concrete

If you want readers to picture the action, picture it first yourself. I visualize my stories as a series of scenes, much as in a play. Each scene opens in a specific location at a specific time. The action unfolds as the characters speak and move about the stage. Then the scene ends and the curtain comes down in preparation for the next scene.

Here's how I transfer the scene to text:

From the *SCBWI Bulletin*, April-May 1998.

The curtain rises. I make sure my readers know right away exactly where and when they are. That way, the scenery will be in place in their mental pictures.

The action unfolds. I see a character move. I describe the movement so the reader can see it too. I hear a character speak. I transcribe the words so the reader can hear it too. Note: I don't *describe* the speeches (indirect quote), *I give the words as the reader would hear them* (direct quote).

If I'm tempted to write something I don't see or hear, I think twice. Can't the characters do something on stage that will do the same job? For instance, my characters usually talk to themselves instead of thinking silently.

The curtain falls. What happens then? *Nothing, until the next scene.* I follow this rule fairly strictly because I write picture books, and the curtain corresponds to page turns. But for any story, action should not stay disembodied very long.

Descriptions of scenery, characters, and action can be extremely sketchy. A reader's imagination is a wonderful thing. Give it a small suggestion and it fills in the rest.

Being Invisible

Some years ago, at the National Storytelling Festival in Jonesborough, Tennessee, I was listening to a tale being told by Connie Regan-Blake, a member of a prominent storytelling duo called the Folktellers. She was performing in a huge tent on a hot day to an audience of about a thousand adults. Her delivery was solid and skilled, but not really striking.

All at once, in the middle of the story, I "woke up" with a shock. For just a few seconds, I had completely forgotten I was sitting in a hot tent with a thousand other people—forgotten even that I was listening to Connie Regan-Blake.

She had drawn me into the story so completely that I was aware of nothing but that story's unfolding *within my own mind.*

That moment taught me that the height of storytelling— oral or written—is when the teller becomes invisible.

Part of becoming invisible is to engage the reader's imagination with concrete images, as discussed earlier. If the imagination is busy enough, it will wrap the reader up in the story and draw attention away from the writer. (In the words of the great and powerful Wizard of Oz, "Never mind that man behind the curtain!")

At the same time, though, the writer must carefully avoid drawing attention back to the text. Here are some things that will "distance" a reader from the story:

Obscurity and ambiguity. The text must be crystal clear, so readers don't have to stop and figure things out. Make your meaning obvious, and never make your readers choose between two possible meanings. Don't skimp on a comma if it's needed to show clearly where one phrase ends and the next begins.

Remember, text is a *linear* medium. Don't make a reader double back to get the meaning of text that came earlier. For instance, readers should never have to wonder who is doing what. Subjects should generally be at the start of sentences. Attributions of dialog should come no later than after the first sentence. If that sentence is a long one, put the attribution between clauses, or even add a short exclamatory sentence in front.

Fancy language and long descriptions. Language should be rhythmic and artful, but at the same time simple and direct. Sophisticated, complex, or gimmicky language becomes the focus of attention.

You might think that extensive description would bring readers deeper into the story, but the opposite is generally true. This is because long descriptive passages break the action. In essence, you're asking your characters to freeze in place until you're done. Readers are more caught up when the action takes place in "real time."

Narrator intrusion. This happens when a writer inserts a personal comment, judgment, or opinion into third-person narrative, or worst of all, addresses the reader directly. Readers at once become acutely aware of the writer lurking behind the words—or in front of them. A single indiscreet adjective can bring a reader up short.

A few writers, like Roald Dahl, can purposely intrude themselves and pull it off wonderfully. Most of us, though, do better to keep the narrative tone strictly objective and let the story speak for itself.

Ironically, when you make your text less visible, your prose may draw less notice and less praise. It may even be criticized as plain. But you'll know better when you see young listeners staring up with wide, glazed eyes.

You'll know that your words are making pictures.

Rhythm and the Readaloud

One of the greatest compliments a reviewer can bestow on a children's story is to call it a "great readaloud." But how does a story come to merit such praise? The secret is *rhythm*—rhythm in language and rhythm in structure.

Rhythm in Language

The primary rhythmic unit of language is the sentence. Children's writers are often told to keep sentences short, but this mostly takes care of itself when we aim at rhythmic vigor. More to the point is to practice these two rules:

1. Reduce the distance between beats.
2. Reduce the number of beats.

A *beat* occurs at every syllable that is "stressed" or "accented." To practice the first rule, choose and arrange your words and phrases so that the smallest number of unaccented syllables falls between accented ones. Try to allow only one or two, and rarely more than three. To follow the second rule, choose and arrange your words and phrases to produce the smallest total number of beats in the sentence.

Of course, just how tight the rhythms should be will depend on the mood you wish to create. For a leisurely, lyrical story, you would allow more unaccented syllables and more

From the *SCBWI Bulletin*, April-May 1996.

beats per sentence. For a lively, active story, you would allow fewer.

The above rules have two familiar corollaries: Delete unnecessary words. And use short words—generally words with one or two syllables, and rarely those with more than three. The primary reason for using short words is not that they're easier to read and understand but that they help the rhythm.

For instance, the difficulty with a word like "difficulty" is that it contains three unaccented syllables. In the previous sentence, this makes a total of five unaccented syllables between the beats on "dif-" and "word." That's all right for a professional article, but not for a story! Better to use a word like "problem," or a phrase like "what's wrong." Other long words, such as "nevertheless," add two beats to the sentence, instead of the single beat from a word like "still."

But length is not the only criterion of word selection. Two words with the same number of syllables often have different rhythms, depending on where the accent falls. "Over" and "above" will each work best in different settings.

Almost as important as selection of words and phrases is arrangement. By changing the order, you might avoid a long string of unaccented syllables or get rid of a beat. It is well worth trying a sentence in several different forms to find the one with the best rhythm.

Arrangement also helps fit your thought into the inherent rhythm of the sentence. The greatest stress in a sentence naturally falls at the end, and the second greatest stress at the beginning. A skilled writer uses this by aiming to place emphasized words and phrases in these positions. Language and grammatical form then support each other, and both are made stronger. With proper sentence construction, a writer seldom needs italics for emphasis.

In regard to rhythm, the most crucial sentence in the story is the final one. This sentence must wind down the story and signal itself as the ending. The most tried-and-true way to achieve this is with a "slow three," as found in "*hap*-pily *ev*-er *af*-ter." Here are examples from my own stories:

But I'll bet he still aims at the heart.
And never a brush stroke in sight.
"At last I've got the willies!"

The paragraph is another important rhythmic unit of language. Just as you aim at minimizing beats in a sentence, try also to minimize the number of sentences in a paragraph. Take out any sentences that aren't essential. See if the thoughts in two sentences can be efficiently merged in a single sentence.

For a picture book, I recommend allowing three sentences per paragraph, and rarely more than four. Allow one or two more if a paragraph combines dialog and narration, but still allow only three for dialog.

As in the sentence, the most important position in the paragraph is at the end, and the second most important is at the beginning. Sentences containing the most important thoughts are best placed in these positions.

Rhythmic interest is achieved in language by both variety and repetition. Sentences should vary in number of beats from one to the next, and paragraphs should vary in number of sentences. Alternatively, you can create interest by rigidly repeating a pattern of beats or sentences.

Variety is also produced by mixing dialog with narration. For a picture book, I recommend making dialog one-third to one-half of your text.

Rhythm in Structure

Plot structure generates a larger rhythm to the story. This structure is made up of one or more *incidents,* which are in turn made up of one or more *scenes.* (I use *scene* in roughly the sense it would be used for a play: a setting with distinct time and location.) With these elements too, interest can be created by both variety and repetition.

Different story ideas require different plot structures, but those with appealing rhythms often follow the folktale's "rule of three." For instance, a simple plot might consist of three central incidents—perhaps of parallel construction—framed by an introduction and a conclusion. Sets of three usually work well rhythmically because they satisfy without becoming wearisome.

Another satisfying rhythm is produced by scenes or incidents alternating between opposites—good and evil, wise and stupid, night and day, cause and effect. Of course, these alternations too can be presented in sets of three.

Scenes and incidents convey stronger rhythms when they are clearly demarcated. This is most important for picture book scenes. The first paragraph should set the relative time and location and launch the action. The last paragraph should wind up the action and convey a sense of what has taken place. This paragraph should end with a punch, often in the form of dialog. If picture book scenes are constructed properly, correct placement of page divisions should be obvious without blank lines or other notation in the manuscript.

Alongside the story's plot structure is its dramatic structure, which bears its own rhythm. Most successful stories follow a similar pattern: Dramatic tension starts at a low level, then rises until the climax point is reached near the end of the story—then plummets back to the starting level as the conflict resolves. But the climb is generally not steady. Progressive rises are separated by shallow dips that act as resting places.

It is the breadth of this rhythm that largely determines the story's impact. The higher the level of dramatic tension you attain, the more memorable your story. Of course, the tension level must not rise too high for the age group.

A writer works with a multitude of rhythms as surely as does a musician or a dancer. By becoming aware of the rhythms and using them effectively, your stories can earn the coveted label of "readaloud."

Researching the Folktale

Folktale retellers are being watched. Editors, reviewers, and librarians are demanding greater authenticity in retellings, along with documentation of sources. And retellers must watch themselves as well, to avoid infringing copyright law.

What it all means is that retellers must conduct more thorough research than ever before, both for sources and for cultural background.

Where Did It Come From?

When you come across a folktale you might like to retell, your first question should be, "Where did this story come from?" Did the author collect the story firsthand? If so, there will probably be some mention of that in an introduction, foreword, or author note.

But most folktales in children's collections are retold from earlier versions. (Often the author was not as careful about copyright law as you should try to be!) Your job then is to trace the story back to its earliest printed source. This is the version that will be most authentic, because someone *did* collect it firsthand.

If you're lucky, the book in which you first read the folktale will have a source note. But usually you'll need to search on your own. And even if a source note is provided,

Updated from the *SCBWI Bulletin*, February-March 1996.

you may be able to find other and possibly better sources than those used by the author.

A word of caution: Many original stories are written in a folktale style, and some may even falsely claim to be folktales. An experienced student of folklore can usually tell the difference, but most people can't. This makes it all the more important to look for an earlier source.

The Long Arm of the Law

Authenticity is not the only reason to search for the earliest printed version. You are also trying to step out of reach of the long arm of the law—the copyright law, that is.

In the United States, changes in that law have made the situation increasingly complex, as well as increasingly unfavorable to retellers. But here are the basics for works originally published in the U.S., for anytime up through the year 2018. (Note: This information is based on copyright law as of 2000. For details and updates, contact the U.S. Copyright Office, Library of Congress, Washington, D.C. 20559, 202-707-3000, http://lcweb.loc.gov/copyright/.)

• **1964 or after.** Anything with a copyright date in this period is still protected.

• **1923 to 1963.** Anything copyrighted in this period *may* still be protected, depending on whether the copyright was ever renewed. The only way to find out is to conduct a copyright search. (Get the Copyright Office's Circular 22, "How to Investigate the Copyright Status of a Work.")

• **1922 or before.** Anything published in this period is definitely out of copyright. Fair game. Free and clear.

What if the work was originally published in another country? If you're publishing in the U.S. yourself, then U.S.

law applies to all works you might wish to use—but the protection given by that law may still differ. Works from some countries are not legally protected at all! For most countries, though, figure that anything published in 1923 or after is protected, while anything published earlier is not.

Many people believe that folktales cannot be copyrighted. It's true that the tale itself is in the public domain, but how the tale is retold belongs to the author. For instance, the author is likely to have named a character, created dialog, or modified a plot incident. Original elements such as these are covered by copyright, and for as long as the story is legally protected, you're not supposed to use them.

To avoid problems, work with at least one version that is no longer in copyright and that you can use as your primary source. If that's not possible, you might work with several distinct versions—retellings from different firsthand sources—in order to reconstruct the tale in generic form.

The Search for Sources

In general, your goal is to find as many sources as possible, and the earliest ones possible. The more sources you have, and the more authentic they are, the better you can see what in the tale is essential, what can or should be modified, and what options are available for manipulating it.

This search for sources will usually include standard folktale bibliographic references. One or more of the following will be on the reference shelf at most larger libraries:

The Storyteller's Sourcebook, Margaret Read MacDonald.
Index to Fairy Tales, Mary Eastman/Norma Ireland. An index to collections.
Annotated Bibliography and Index to Single Editions, Elsie Ziegler. An index to picture books.

The Types of the Folktale, Antti Aarne and Stith Thompson.
The Motif-Index of Folk-Literature, Stith Thompson.

The first two sources will be the most useful to retellers. The two Stith Thompson indexes are best suited to multilingual scholars, but you would do well to study his one-volume overview, *The Folktale.*

Often you will find that the retellers of tales of a particular geographic area have mostly based their work on a mere handful of older, authoritative, adult sources—sometimes on only a single book. Such a book may have been compiled, for instance, by a British resident of an African colony at the turn of the century, or by a north European nationalist scholar searching for his literary heritage in the late 1900s.

You can identify these treasurehouses by looking for works often cited in source notes. Many are mentioned in Thompson's *The Folktale* and in the *Funk and Wagnalls Standard Dictionary of Folklore, Mythology, and Legend.* It also pays to comb the shelves of major public and university libraries.

Nowadays, much of my own bibliographic research is done from the comfort of my home, connecting to major library catalogs online. Most university libraries now offer catalog access via direct dial-up, telnet, and/or the Web. My favorite service is MELVYL (www.melvyl.ucop.edu, or via www.cdlib.org), which catalogs the collective book holdings of the University of California campuses. I can search the catalog by title, author, subject, language, or any combination of these. When I find a likely title, I order it from my local public library as an interlibrary loan.

Of course, when you find a prime source, you may find not only an earlier version of the folktale you've seen, but also new folktales to consider.

The Quest for Context

Traditional storytellers in other cultures don't need to pause and explain details of custom or tradition found in their tales. They are telling their stories to people who know those details quite well. Retellers, on the other hand, are writing for people who may have no inkling of them. So retellers must make sure to understand the cultural context and then relay it to their readers.

One obvious but good place to start for background information is the *Encyclopedia Britannica*. For information on foreign customs, travel guides are good, and so are travelogues written before the days of Third World modernization. You might search out an immigrant for answers to some of your questions.

A fair amount of my own background research has now moved onto the World Wide Web. You can often unearth highly useful but obscure material through a search at AltaVista (www.altavista.com) or another search engine. For instance, when I retold the Chinese legend of White Snake, I was able to locate online photos of West Lake, one of the story settings.

The Web is also a good place to find people who can answer questions. For example, I needed to name the heroine of a folktale from the Chagga tribe of Mount Kilimanjaro. I managed to find the home page of a Chagga tribesman teaching at Pennsylvania State University! By email, he suggested several names, one of which was perfect.

Internet newsgroups and email discussion lists can be helpful as well. Many are dedicated to specific countries, cultures, or religions. When I queried an Iranian newsgroup about the tale of Mushkil Gusha, one respondent in the U.S.

supplied a complete variant he'd heard often from his grandmother while growing up in southern Iran!

Don't Forget to Write

You've done the research and retold the tale. But don't leave it there. Follow up by writing a great author note. Impress us with your obscure sources. Enlighten us with interesting cultural details. Maybe even tell us how to say the names. Reviewers and librarians will give you higher marks, and your books will be more useful in the classroom.

Go ahead and show off a little. You've earned it.

In Praise of Post-its

Another submission, another cover letter. You sit down to compose those very special words of introduction that will entice the editor to wholeheartedly consider your manuscript. A quarter of an hour later, you may have a masterpiece that says little more than "Enclosed is my manuscript."

On the other end, the editor rips open the envelope and spends a quarter of a *minute*—or less—glancing at the cover letter. It is then shoved aside and forgotten as she turns to the manuscript.

Multiply that by perhaps hundreds of submissions over the course of a career. Is it worth the effort? In most cases, no.

Is there an alternative? Yes!

I have become an avid proponent of the lowly Post-it®. This miraculous device can save enormous amounts of both time and paper. In most cases, everything you need to say can fit handily in three inches square.

Here are some favorite notes I've used regularly with editors, both familiar and unknown.

- "Hope you like this!"
- "Thanks for your comments on _____. This one may suit you better."

From *Once Upon a Time,* Spring 1993.
"Post-it" is a registered trademark of Minnesota Mining and Manufacturing Company (3M).

- "You've seen this one before, but I've revised it."
- "I'm a member of SCBWI."
- "This appeared in *Cricket*."
- "Congratulations on your new position!"

It's possible to send a manuscript with *no* cover message of any kind, but I don't advise it. Editors are not machines. They value personal contact, and making this contact is a prime purpose of the cover message. A Post-it actually works *better* for this than a standard cover letter, because it is less stuffy.

But what if you really *do* have more to say than can fit on a Post-it—like a long list of publications or other impressive qualifications?

I recommend an author flyer, brief resumé, or other type of information sheet. Develop a single-sheet form that can be included with all submissions. This can tell a great deal *more* than a cover letter. It can give the editor a sense of you as a person, and may also help her to "sell" the manuscript to others at her house.

So, escape the enslavement of the cover letter and pick up a pack of Post-its. With the time you save, maybe you can write another story!

The Picture Book Query

Note: A sample picture book query follows this article.

Picture book query? Isn't that almost a contradiction in terms? You're not supposed to send queries for picture books, are you?

No, you're not. But I did. And as a result of my query campaign, I found my dream editor and had four stories accepted—in just five months!

It was almost an accident. In 1990, I had a retold folktale from India that had been rejected by nearly everyone. A friend suggested I try publishers in Britain and Australia. So I compiled a mailing list and got ready to send out copies.

Then I figured up the cost of overseas mailing. "Well," I thought, "maybe I'll do more research first." So I decided to send queries. But if I was querying for *one* story, why not for others? I put together a descriptive list of my available manuscripts, all on one page, and sent it off.

At the time, I was very frustrated about my writing career. I had sold one picture book story, but the publisher hadn't taken any more. And though a number of editors were writing me personal notes, they weren't buying. I was convinced my stories were publishable, if only I could find the right editor.

The query form I'd come up with seemed to me a pretty handy tool. It occurred to me that a query campaign to U.S. publishers might flush out that special editor I needed.

From the *SCBWI Bulletin,* September-October 1992.

So I made another mailing list and began sending queries to editors. The form itself was printed out on my letterhead, with the title "Picture Book Texts Available." Each story was described in two to four lines, with a place for a checkmark beside it.

At the bottom, I had two choices for checking: "Please send the manuscripts indicated," and "Not interested, because _____." Then came blank lines for the editor's and publisher's names. (I found out it's a good idea to fill in the these names yourself. I got an unsigned request for three stories, and it took me four months to track it down.)

At the top right of each copy, I stuck a Post-it saying something along the lines of "Would you like to see any of these? I have sold to _____ and _____." With the query sheet went a list of my publications and a self-addressed, stamped envelope.

In the course of working with this new tool, I discovered a number of nice points about it. Consider these:

• Your coverage of the market can be broader. You can safely submit a query to every likely publisher at once—even to multiple imprints within the same house. And the low cost of querying makes this affordable.

• Your coverage of the market can be deeper. If a query comes back with a negative response from one editor—or if it doesn't come back within a reasonable time at all—you can query another editor at the same house or imprint. You probably wouldn't risk that with a manuscript.

• The editor sees you're a serious writer with a stock of stories—not someone with a single manuscript written ten years ago.

• The editor can respond to the focus and range of your work as a whole. You are more likely to connect with editors interested in your *type* of story, rather than in a single story that happened to catch their eye. (Connecting with the wrong editor can prevent you from finding a more suitable editor at the same house.)

• The editor saves you the work of deciding the best manuscripts to send! And you gain other hints about the pattern and depth of that editor's interest. For instance, if she selects one story that's different from all the rest, then maybe that editor isn't for you. (If one of your stories has appeared in a magazine, I suggest you leave it off the list or don't mention the fact. Many editors will simply select anything published—so you learn nothing about their own preferences.)

• The responses taken together may show you which of your story ideas have the most potential for success. This may help you in selecting ideas for future projects.

• You don't have to send the stories requested! If an editor requests one you've already sent to another imprint at the same house, or if too many editors have requested that story, you can send a similar one, along with an explanation. You can also send *additional* stories you think the editor might like, based on their response pattern.

• Whatever you send now is "solicited." It stays out of the slush pile, and may gain a slight edge in consideration. If it is later rejected, you still are more likely to get helpful comments.

• If you do *not* get comments when rejected, you have no commitment to the editor. Her initial response to your query isn't considered the beginning of a personal correspondence. So no one will mind if you contact a different editor at that house.

One expected advantage did not materialize. I thought that responses to queries would come back much faster than responses to manuscripts. Wishful thinking! Most editors still took months to reply.

But what about results? Within half a year, I sent 56 queries to editors at 40 major U.S. houses or imprints. Ten queries got no response at all. Of the responses, 26 were negative and 20 were positive. (Several responding editors advised me not to query for picture books. At least one of those editors also asked to see a story!)

The 20 positive responses included requests for a total of 43 manuscript copies. The stories I sent garnered personal notes from eleven editors. Eight of the notes were encouraging enough to place the editor on my mailing list for future submissions.

But the best result came just four months into my campaign. After reading two of my stories, the head of an imprint at a major house called and offered a contract for one of them, with a good royalty and a hefty advance. A month later, she asked me to set aside three more manuscripts for upcoming contracts.

I had found my editor!

Aaron Shepard

P. O. Box 555   Hometown, California 55555 USA   555-555-5555

Picture Book Texts Available

____ *The Legend of Lightning Larry.* Original tale of a gunfighter with a huge smile and a gun that shoots bolts of light instead of bullets. Can Larry save the town of Brimstone from Evil-Eye McNeevil's outlaw gang?

____ *The Legend of Slappy Hooper.* Tall tale from Depression-era Chicago of the world's biggest, fastest, bestest sign painter. Trouble is, he's *too good*—his pictures keep coming to life.

____ *The Gifts of Wali Dad.* Indian and Pakistani tale of a humble grasscutter who tries again and again to give away unwanted wealth—only to receive ever-greater wealth in return.

____ *The Baker's Dozen.* Legend from colonial America about a self-righteous baker who gets a lesson in generosity from an old woman and Saint Nicholas.

____ *The Enchanted Storks.* Classic Middle Eastern tale of a caliph of Bagdad and his vizier who try a spell that changes them into storks, then find they can't change back.

____ *Master Man.* Nigerian tale of a man who boasts he is the strongest in the world—until he meets the *real* strongest man. Will he end up as dessert, or can anyone save him?

____ *Mop Top.* Norwegian tale of a wild princess and her wilder adventures. Babies grow on trees, troll girls cavort, heads pop off, and butts are bopped.

____ *The Boy Who Wanted the Willies.* A Grimm brothers tale of a ridiculously fearless boy in a thoroughly haunted castle. Will he ever get the willies?

____ *The Lady of Stavoren.* Dutch legend of how the arrogant pride of a rich lady merchant—and her quest for the most precious thing in the world—brought ruin to a prosperous seaport.

____ *Kings for Breakfast!* Tall tale from India of one king who grants every request, and another who is fried, eaten, and magically restored daily to earn gold for the poor. Which of them is more generous?

____ Please send the manuscripts indicated.

____ Not interested, because _____

EDITOR: _____

HOUSE: _____

AS@aaronshep.com • www.aaronshep.com

Picture Book Query

10 Ways to Promote a First Book

Your first book may be a masterpiece, but first books have a nasty way of getting ignored. Bookstores may not bother to order it. If they do carry it, store personnel may not know it's on the shelf. Another problem is that, if your book appeals to special audiences, your publisher may not know how to reach them.

My own first picture book was *Savitri: A Tale of Ancient India* (Whitman, 1992), a retold 3,000-year-old story of a princess who outwits the god of death to save her husband's life. Here are ten methods I used to boost recognition of the book.

1. Throw a book party. I mailed out 200 invitations to friends, booksellers, librarians, reviewers, and everyone else in my community I wanted to let know about *Savitri*. I didn't expect them all to come, but I at least made them aware of the book. The party cost me nothing, because I held it at my home, asked friends to bring potluck desserts or beverages, and sold books during the party.

2. Visit local bookstores and libraries. I showed the book to my local booksellers and librarians and encouraged them to order it. From this came several invitations for storytelling/signings, plus a bookstore offer to host receptions for future books.

3. Compile a list of reviewers. Usually your publisher will ask you for a list of periodicals that would be especially

---

From the *SCBWI Bulletin,* June-July 1994.

interested in your book. If the book appeals to one or more specialized audiences, this is particularly important. From standard library references such as *The Encyclopedia of Associations* and *Ulrich's International Periodicals Directory*, I made a list of Hindu, yoga, and Indo-American publications, including newsletters of major organizations. Having been a professional storyteller, I also listed storytelling publications and children's radio shows.

4. Compile a list of retailers. Your publisher may ask also for a list of bookstores for special notification. Again, this is most important for a specialized book. From telephone directories at my library, I made a list of bookstores specializing in Eastern religion, along with a smattering of educational resource, feminist, New Age, and museum bookstores. Small, specialized booksellers are often overlooked by publishers' sales representatives, but can be major sales outlets if your book meets their needs.

Normally, stores on your list are notified by the publisher, but I took care of this myself, so I could add personal notes. In an age of computerized mailings, a scribbled note gets attention!

5. Offer school visits. My first school visit came just a couple of months after publication, from someone on my review copy list. After that, I sent notices of my availability to a number of schools, along with information on me and my book. (Such mailings work best if you follow up with phone calls.)

6. Produce an instructional aid. This is something for use in the classroom in conjunction with your book. Drawing on my experience in reader's theater, I produced a script adaptation of *Savitri*. My hope was that teachers who used the script would also want the picture book to share with students.

As it happened, Whitman's promotions director declined to use the script in the publisher's promotional efforts. But it is now posted on my Web site (www.aaronshep.com) and is also included in my published collection of reader's theater adaptations, *Stories on Stage* (H. W. Wilson, 1993).

7. Join organizations. In order to link up with people who buy and promote books, I joined the Association of Booksellers for Children, the Northern California Children's Booksellers Association, the Association of Children's Librarians (for the San Francisco Bay area), the California Reading Association, and the Sacramento Area Reading Association.

The newsletters of these organizations are very informative, and the meetings are great places to get known. For instance, I arranged to read *Savitri* at a monthly meeting of the Northern California Children's Booksellers Association—in this way reaching many of the area's children's booksellers at one time.

8. Attend events. In the half year after *Savitri's* publication, I attended—at my own expense—the American Booksellers Association convention in Anaheim, the American Library Assocation convention in San Francisco, the Celebration of Children's Literature at the University of California, Berkeley, and the Northern California Booksellers Association convention in Oakland. At each of these events, I found many opportunities to show the book to people who could help it along. (I also made friends and had a lot of fun.)

9. Write an article. In case you haven't noticed, this article too was meant as a way to promote the book—as well as a way to share useful information.

10. Work on your next book. There is no end to the ways you can promote a book, or to the time you can spend doing it. But the very best way is to work on your next one. Repeated publication builds your reputation and sales potential better than anything else. So, promote your work, but don't forget that your readers are waiting for more!

Promo Pieces for the Children's Author

Note: Sample author and book flyers follow this article.

Effective promotional pieces will support your writing career in any number of ways. You don't need to hire someone to produce them, or even buy special software. All you need is your regular word processing program, a good printer, and an inexpensive scanner.

Here are some of the basic promo pieces you might find useful:

Author flyer. This general flyer contains all the most important information about you and what you do and how to contact you, and projects the image you wish to convey. You'll find many uses for it. For example, you can include it with your manuscript submissions to editors who don't yet know you well.

Book flyers. You'll need these as a quick way to convey all essential information about your books. A flyer can feature one book or many. Include scanned graphics from the book covers or interior art, and also comments from reviewers.

Info sheets. It's usually quicker and easier to send someone a sheet of information than to try to convey detailed information over the phone or by letter. My own assortment of info sheets includes "School Visits," "Library Visits,"

Updated from the *SCBWI Bulletin*, October-November 1995.

"Conference Appearances," "Talks and Workshops," "Book Sales and Ordering," and "Fees and Expenses."

Author profile. This is a more in-depth look than in the author flyer. Educational publications might want to publish this as an article, and teachers can use it to help prepare students for your school visit. Include personal history, a description of your writing process, and anything else that will make you come alive in the mind of the reader.

Instructional aids. Teachers may be more likely to use your book if there are classroom activities to go with it. Some authors with strong educational backgrounds prepare detailed lesson plans. For each of my own picture books, I prepare a free reader's theater script for easy classroom dramatization.

Autographed bookmarks. Create a sheet that has several signed bookmarks on it, for photocopying and cutting into individual bookmarks. Send it ahead to schools you visit, so that even students who don't buy books can have something to take home.

Photos. Keep a good stock of your portrait photo for sending to event organizers. You might wind up in the newspaper! A size of 4" X 6" is as large as you'll need, and color is fine, even if the photo will be reproduced in black-and-white.

Others. No doubt you'll think of other promo pieces suited to you and your work. Among my own are a one-page handout of my best-loved story (from a picture book now out of print), a "portrait poster" with a cartoon sketch of me by the illustrator of two of my books, and a flyer about my Web site.

For printing your pieces, a laser printer is best. Though more expensive than an inkjet and limited to black-and-white, it is much cheaper to operate and faster and produces more professional results.

Some of your pieces may be double-sided. If you have trouble running your paper through a laser printer a second time, try this trick: With your "Page Layout" options, set your word processor to print the second page upside down and backwards. Then feed the paper itself backwards into the printer.

Of course, nowadays there's an alternative to print and paper: You can post your pieces on the Web. In fact, a Web site can have many more promo pieces and of a much greater variety than is practical or even possible in print form. Still, you'll always need print versions of essential pieces to mail or hand out. (For a look at my own promo pieces for the Web, visit www.aaronshep.com.)

A final tip: Most promo pieces must be kept current with up-to-date information, and this can take a substantial amount of your time. So be selective and create only the pieces you need. Promotion is worthwhile, but not if it keeps you from writing!

Aaron Shepard
Children's Author

Aaron Shepard is the award-winning author of *The Sea King's Daughter, The Baker's Dozen, The Legend of Lightning Larry*, and many more picture books from major publishers. His work also appears often in *Cricket Magazine.*

Aaron's specialty is retelling folktales and other traditional literature from around the world. His work has been honored by the American Library Association, the National Council for the Social Studies, and the American Folklore Society. His stories are enjoyed by the entire range of elementary grades—as well as by adults—and are perfect for reading aloud.

When Aaron isn't writing, he loves to visit young people in elementary schools and libraries across the country and beyond. Drawing on his past experience in professional storytelling and reader's theater, he mesmerizes young audiences with dramatic readings of his published stories and works-in-progress, and also offers frank insights into a writer's life and process.

On the World Wide Web, Aaron maintains an extensive collection of resources and treats for teachers, librarians, parents, storytellers, children's writers, and young people. His site has been viewed by over a quarter million visitors and currently draws about 5,000 visitors a week.

Aaron is also considered a prime resource for reader's theater. He promotes this innovative teaching tool through his Web page and his acclaimed script collection from H. W. Wilson, *Stories on Stage.*

An acclaimed author with real kid appeal, Aaron takes pleasure in sharing the magic of story.

"A gifted writer."—Jane Yolen, in *Parabola*

"Aaron Shepard! Wow! What a treasure chest of stories you have to entertain and delight us! No matter what you do, you are always entertaining and enriching."—Jan Lieberman, Literature Consultant and Publisher, *TNT Newsletter*

Aaron Shepard
P.O. Box 555 • Hometown, CA 55555
555-555-5555 • AS@aaronshep.com
www.aaronshep.com————| Please visit! |

Author Flyer

The Legend of
Lightning Larry

By Aaron Shepard
Pictures by Toni Goffe

No outlaw could draw as fast as Lightning Larry. But what really terrified those bad men was that peculiar gun of his. It didn't shoot bullets. It shot light. And Larry always aimed for the heart.

Can Larry save the town of Brimstone from Evil-Eye McNeevil's outlaw gang? Find out in this rip-roaring tale of a cowboy with a huge smile and a hankering for lemonade.

> "A tall-tale superhero for our time…. Shepard tells his tale with such exuberant good humor, and explores the consequences with such comical logic, that the moral doesn't detract from the fun. A readaloud that could lighten up classes well up in the elementary grades."—*Kirkus Reviews*, 3/1/93

> "Pass out the bandanas and dig out the spittoon. Read this story in an old-timer's voice, and everyone will have a good time."—Chris Sherman, American Library Association *Booklist*, 3/1/93

> "Perfect for telling or reading out loud."—Katy Rydell, *Stories*, Spring 1993

> "A rib-tickler… Kids will enjoy acting this out as readers theatre."—Jan Lieberman, *TNT*, Spring 1993

Scribners, 1993, 32 pages, full-color illustrations, LC #91-43779, ISBN 0-684-19433-3, $14.95. Preschool–grade 6.

Book Flyer #1

Picture Books by
Aaron Shepard

The Sea King's Daughter

Illustrated by Gennady Spirin. A classic legend of Russia about a young musician invited to play in the Sea King's palace, where he's offered more than riches. "Emotionally authentic prose and jewel-like illustrations make this an exquisite volume."—*Publishers Weekly* (starred review)

- 1998 American Library Association Notable Children's Books
- 1998 NCSS/CBC Notable Children's Trade Books in the Field of Social Studies
- 1997 Aesop Accolade (American Folklore Society)
- 1998 Honor Title, *Storytelling World* Awards
- 1997 *New York Times* Best Illustrated Books
- 1997 *Cincinnati Enquirer* Best Illustrated Children's Books
- *American Bookseller* Pick of the Lists
- Featured on "CBS This Morning"

Atheneum, 1997, 40 pages, LC #96-3391, ISBN 0-689-80759-7, $17. Grades 2 and up.

The Baker's Dozen

Illustrated by Wendy Edelson. A holiday legend from colonial America, in which a self-righteous baker gets a lesson in generosity from an old woman and Saint Nicholas. "The good will of Saint Nick resonates in this tale."—*Publishers Weekly*
- *American Bookseller* Pick of the Lists

Atheneum, 1995, 32 pages, LC #92-38261, ISBN 0-689-80298-6, $15.00. Grades K-7.

The Gifts of Wali Dad

Illustrated by Daniel San Souci. A charming tale from India and Pakistan about a humble grasscutter who tries again and again to give away unwanted wealth—only to receive ever-greater wealth in return. "An irresistible hero."—*Kirkus*
- 1995 Aesop Accolade (American Folklore Society)
- 1996 Honor Title, *Storytelling World* Awards
- *American Bookseller* Pick of the Lists
- Children's Book-of-the-Month Club selection

Atheneum, 1995, 32 pages, LC #94-14175, ISBN 0-684-19445-7, $16.00. All ages.

The Legend of Lightning Larry

Illustrated by Toni Goffe. An original tale of a gunfighter with a huge smile and a gun that shoots bolts of light instead of bullets. Can Larry save the town of Brimstone from Evil-Eye McNeevil's outlaw gang? "A tall-tale superhero for our time... A readaloud that could lighten up classes well up in the elementary grades."—*Kirkus*

Scribners/Atheneum, 1993, 32 pages, LC #91-43779, ISBN 0-684-19433-3, $14.95. Preschool–grade 6.

More ➡

Book Flyer #2—Front

Savitri: A Tale of Ancient India

Illustrated by Vera Rosenberry. Through ingenuity and strength of will, the princess Savitri saves her husband from the god of death. From India's national epic, the *Mahabharata*. "Unique and noteworthy... Like ancient myth, [Shepard's interpretation] renews deep strains of potential within the reader."—*Publishers Weekly*

Albert Whitman, 1992, 40 pages, reinforced, LC #91-16591, ISBN 0-8075-7251-9, $16.95. Grades 2-7.

The Enchanted Storks

Illustrated by Alisher Dianov. A classic tale of Baghdad about a caliph and his vizier who try a spell that changes them into storks, then find they can't change back. "Gorgeous panoply."—*School Library Journal*
    • Children's Book-of-the-Month Club selection

Clarion, 1995, 32 pages, LC #93-41540, ISBN 0-395-65377-0, $14.95. Grades 2 and up.

Master Maid

Illustrated by Pauline Ellison. A lively tale of Norway in which Leif goes to work for the troll and only a remarkable young woman can save him from his foolishness. "Expertly told.... An ideal choice for telling or reading aloud."—*School Library Journal*

Dial, 1997, 32 pages, LC #94-37527, ISBN 0-8037-1821-7, ISBN 0-8037-1822-5 (library), $14.99. All ages.

The Legend of Slappy Hooper

Illustrated by Toni Goffe. A tall tale from mid-century America about the world's biggest, fastest, bestest sign painter. Trouble is, he's *too good*—his pictures keep coming to life. But all is not lost, for Slappy has friends in high places. "Well told, amiably satirical."—*Kirkus*

Scribners/Atheneum, 1993, 32 pages, LC #92-18153, ISBN 0-684-19535-6, $14.95. Grades K-6.

The Maiden of Northland

Illustrated by Carol Schwartz. An epic tale of two heroes who vie with magic for the hand of a sorceress's daughter. A free verse retelling from Finland's *Kalevala*. "Retains a sense of majestic rhythm... Unusual and appealing."—*School Library Journal*
    • 1996 Aesop Accolade (American Folklore Society)

Atheneum, 1996, 40 pages, LC #95-78300, ISBN 0-689-80485-7, $16. Grades 4 and up.

Still to Come...

The Crystal Heart: A Vietnamese Legend, illus. by Joseph Fiedler, Atheneum, Fall 1998.
Forty Fortunes: A Tale of Iran, illus. by Alisher Dianov, Clarion, 1999.
Master Man: A Tall Tale of Nigeria, illus. by David Wisniewski, Lothrop.
The King o' the Cats, Atheneum.
The Princess Mouse: A Tale of Finland, Atheneum.

For more information, visit www.aaronshep.com

7.0

Book Flyer #2—Back

Info for Author Days

To make your school visit enjoyable and effective in promoting reading, a school must know what you need, offer, and expect. With so many details involved, you can simplify matters by creating a standard info sheet providing all important information.

Here's what the sheet should include:

Contact info: Your name, address, phone, email, Web page, etc.

General: Can the school make arrangements with you directly, or should it first contact your publisher? Do you need written confirmation of the date and fee, or perhaps a signed contract? Specify anything else you'll need in advance—schedule, school contact info, directions. Do you require more than one day of visits for a long-distance engagement?

Recommendation: In most cases, it's simplest to allow schools to deal with you directly. Written confirmation is good, but you probably don't need a signed contract—especially if you require the school to directly purchase any tickets.

Author presentations. What grade levels are you willing to present to? Do you limit the size of the audience? How long is your presentation? What does it consist of? Do you offer different presentations for specialized needs?

Equipment. Tell what the school must supply for your presentation—P.A. system, A.V. equipment, table, water.

Taping. Do you allow audio or video taping of your presentation? Do you limit distribution of the recording?

Recommendation: Since one of your objects is maximum exposure, taping should generally be welcome—as long as the recording isn't sold. With some kinds of presentations, though, you must judge whether a video might be used in place of your future live appearances.

Schedule. How many presentations are you willing to make in a day? Can the day be split between two schools? Do you offer partial days for a reduced fee? How much break time do you need between presentations? How much time for lunch?

Recommendation: Many authors limit the number of presentations to three, though if you can manage four, it will be easier for two schools to share you. In this time of tight school budgets, it makes sense to offer local schools the less expensive alternative of a "half-day" of two presentations only. This also can let you avoid rush-hour driving!

Escort. Would you like an escort assigned to you for the day?

Recommendation: An escort is nice, but sometimes difficult for the school to arrange.

Student preparation. Do you request that students be made familiar with your work ahead of time? Have you specific suggestions on how to do this?

Recommendation: You should *require* advance preparation as a condition of your visit. Specify this during your initial contact with the school. Though such a requirement is impossible to enforce, it can make a big difference in what is done with the students beforehand—and this preparation in turn is what most determines the quality of your visit. Ideally, your visit should be merely the capstone of an extended experience for the students.

Book sales. Do you request that your books be offered for sale to the students before and/or during your visit? Can you supply the books yourself, or should the school make other arrangements?

Recommendation: Book sales too should be a prior condition of your visit, and should be discussed at first contact. They benefit not only you but the students as well, who will gain much more from your visit if they carry home something concrete. Selling should start before your visit, probably with an order form sent home to parents. It's usually best *not* to supply books yourself, because the school may have little incentive to sell them! Instead, ask the school to order from your publisher or another supplier. As an alternative, the school can request a local bookseller to handle sales.

Autographing. Do you limit your autographing to books? Will you need the names for autographing written out for you? Are you willing to remain after school to finish?

Recommendation: If you don't strictly limit your autographing to books, you will wind up signing an assortment of sheets of paper that students thrust before you. One alternative is to provide the school with a sheet of autographed bookmarks for copying and distribution. This also ensures that those students who can't afford books will not go home empty-handed.

Adult presentations. Do you offer presentations for teachers or parents that can be scheduled after school or the evening before? Do you charge extra for this?

Recommendation: Be sure to require that your books be sold at any such presentation.

Publicity. Would you appreciate your visit publicized in local media? Are you willing to grant interviews?

Recommendation: Of course!

Meals, lodging, transportation. Describe any special requirements—specific foods, nonsmoking facilities, favorite mode of travel. Are you willing to eat and/or sleep in a home? If the school pays expenses, must it do so directly, or can it reimburse you later?

Recommendation: To avoid financial burden and stress, it's best to have the school handle as many expenses directly as possible. This is especially true for large expenses like airline tickets and hotel bills. The school may protest its procedural difficulties, but it can usually find a way if you insist.

Financial. When should you be paid?

Recommendation: This should be before you leave the school, if possible. You can also state your fee here, but I recommend having a separate sheet with fees for all types of presentations. For a full-day visit by an author with a major publisher, a typical starting fee is $500 plus any long-distance expenses.

Other materials. It's handy to include on the sheet a list of other materials you'll be providing in advance to the visited school. Possibilities include author flyer, book flyer, Web page flyer, book sales and ordering info sheet, author profile, autographed bookmark sheet, educational aids, and author photos. (For more information on these, see the earlier article in this book, "Promo Pieces for the Children's Author.")

Have no illusions. Just because you tell a school what you want doesn't mean you'll get it. Like most of us, educators are busy people who may fail to absorb much of what they read, and may forget much of the rest. But by providing your information in an efficient format, you'll at least increase the chances that your author day will be both productive and fun—and you may even earn the school's thanks for making its job that much easier.

APPENDIX

Resources

Books and Periodicals

Market Guide

Children's Writer's & Illustrator's Market, Writer's Digest, annual. Addresses, contact names, and submission guidelines for book publishers, magazines, and almost anything else you might be looking for. Also has much practical advice about the business of writing, plus interviews with prominent people in the field. If you want to buy a market guide, this is it.

Writing Guides

Writing and Publishing Books for Children in the 1990s: The Inside Story from the Editor's Desk, by Olga Litowinsky, Walker, 1992. By a prominent children's book editor. Editors almost always know more of the business than writers do!

The Art of Writing for Children: Skills and Techniques of the Craft, by Connie C. Epstein, Archon, 1991. By a children's book editor and columnist for the *SCBWI Bulletin.*

How to Write a Children's Book and Get It Published, by Barbara Seuling, Macmillan, 1991 (revised edition). A good general introduction.

Writing Books for Young People, by James Giblin, The Writer, 1995 (revised edition). By a children's editor and author, with a specialty in nonfiction.

The Way to Write for Children, by Joan Aiken, St. Martin's, 1982. A quirky and inspirational classic. By the author of The Wolves Chronicles series and much more.

Writing Books for Children, by Jane Yolen, The Writer, 1989. By a prolific and versatile writer with specialties in fantasy and folklore.

How to Write and Sell Children's Picture Books, by Jean E. Karl, Writer's Digest, 1994. A good introduction from a writer's standpoint, by a venerable children's book editor.

Writing with Pictures: How to Write and Illustrate Children's Books, by Uri Shulevitz, Watson-Guptil, 1985. An approach to the picture book, by one of the foremost writer-illustrators today.

How to Write, Illustrate, and Design Children's Books, by Frieda Gates, Library Research Associates, 1986. For illustrators and writer-illustrators. Detailed, specific, practical.

Writing for Young Adults, by Sherry Garland, Writer's Digest, 1998. By a popular young adult author.

The Elements of Style, by William Strunk, Jr., and E. B. White, Allyn & Bacon, 1995 (third edition). How to write simply and directly. This classic should be an early read for almost every children's writer.

The Comic Toolbox: How to Be Funny Even If You're Not, by John Vorhaus, Silman-James, 1994. Helps develop your comic sense by providing patterns and models. The chapter "The Comic Throughline," though focused on screenplays, applies as well to the structure of novels and is alone worth the price of the book.

A Writer's Guide to a Children's Book Contract, by Mary Flower, Fern Hill Books, 385 Atlantic Avenue, Brooklyn, NY 11217, USA, 1988. Though not much to look at and dated in some ways, this is the only book on the subject—and it does a good job. For the U.S. only. Mary Flower is a contracts lawyer specializing in children's books, as well as a columnist for the *SCBWI Bulletin.*

An Author's Guide to Children's Book Promotion, by Susan Salzman Raab, Raab Associates, 1999. Tips and resource listings from a prominent children's book publicist and columnist for the *SCBWI Bulletin.*

How to Capture Live Authors and Bring Them to Your Schools, by David Melton, Landmark Editions, 1986. Though meant for schools that are organizing author visits, this can also help authors know what to expect and what to ask for.

Writer Reference

The Synonym Finder, by J. I. Rodale, Warner Books, 1991 (revised edition). Every writer needs a thesaurus to help find the best choice of words. But if you're using any thesaurus other than this one, chuck it. Rodale's is so far ahead, there really isn't any competition. More than 1,000,000 synonyms!

Merriam-Webster's Standard American Style Manual, Merriam-Webster, 1994. Style manuals contain rules for punctuation, capitalization, grammar, and so on. Each publisher uses a particular style manual to ensure consistency within and among its publications, and editors follow them religiously. The Merriam-Webster is the best for writers because it is aimed at general use rather than at professional editors.

For instance, instead of telling you just one way to do things, it tells you the rules as most often followed by today's editors, then notes all common variants. You'll also find descriptions of proofreading symbols, editorial processes, and more. Studying this manual will help make your submissions more professional and easier to edit—which makes you look good!

Folktale Reference

The Folktale, by Stith Thompson, University of California, 1978 (reprinted from Holt, Rinehart and Winston, 1946). A fascinating scholarly overview of basic tale types and how they are distributed around the world. It also explains Thompson's research tools, the *Type Index* and the *Motif Index*, which you may never use directly but will see many references to and should understand.

Index to Fairy Tales, published by Faxon, several volumes, through 1973. These are indexes of folktale retellings found in story collections. Invaluable for tracking down different versions of a story. Though in print, they are terribly expensive, so find them in the reference section of your library.

The Storyteller's Sourcebook, by Margaret Read MacDonald, Neal-Schuman/Gale, 1982. Another index of folktale retellings, also invaluable—and also expensive enough so you'll want to find it in the reference section of your library. An update volume is in progress.

Periodicals

All listings below are U.S.

SCBWI Bulletin. Official publication of the Society of Children's Book Writers and Illustrators. Bimonthly.

>8271 Beverly Blvd.
>Los Angeles, CA 90048
>323-782-1010
>www.scbwi.org/bulletin.htm

Once Upon A Time: A Support Magazine for Children's Writers and Illustrators. Especially for beginners. Quarterly.

>553 Winston Ct.
>St. Paul, MN 55118
>651-457-6223
>http://members.aol.com/ouatmag/

Publishers Weekly. Includes ongoing coverage of children's book publishing and related fields. Also a major review journal. Extremely expensive, but worth it. A semiannual children's book announcement issue—available also individually—includes nearly every children's book to be published in the next half year, listed by publisher.

>800-278-2991
>www.publishersweekly.com

Other major review media, to be found at many libraries:

>American Library Association *Booklist*
>*School Library Journal*
>*Horn Book*
>*Bulletin of the Center for Children's Books*
>*Kirkus Reviews*
>*Book Links*

Organizations

Children's writers are wise to become familiar not only with the field of writing but also with the professionals who support children's books: booksellers, educators, librarians. All listings here are U.S.

Society of Children's Book Writers and Illustrators (SCBWI). Bi-monthly bulletin, market directories, annual conference, regional branches. Join this!!!!!!!!

> 8271 Beverly Blvd.
> Los Angeles, CA 90048
> 323-782-1010
> info@scbwi.org
> www.scbwi.org

American Booksellers Association (ABA). Annual convention (as part of Book Expo America), publications, mailing lists, some regional affiliates, the national BookSense campaign and Web site.

> 828 S. Broadway
> Tarrytown, NY 10591
> 800-637-0037
> info@bookweb.org
> www.bookweb.org

Association of Booksellers for Children (ABC). Newsletter, mailing list, some regional affiliates.

4412 Chowen Avenue South, #303
Minneapolis, MN 55410
800-421-1665
www.abfc.com

American Library Association (ALA). Annual convention, publications, mailing lists, state affiliates.

50 East Huron St.
Chicago, IL 60611
800-545-2433
ala@ala.org
www.ala.org

American Association of School Librarians (AASL). A division of the American Library Association. Conferences, publications, email discussion lists.

50 East Huron St.
Chicago, IL 606711
800-545-2433 X4389
aasl@ala.org
www.ala.org/aasl

International Reading Association (IRA). Elementary school teachers, other educators, some librarians. Annual convention, publications, mailing lists, state and local affiliates.

800 Barksdale Rd.
P.O. Box 8139
Newark, DE 19714
800-336-7323
pubinfo@reading.org
www.reading.org

National Council of Teachers of English (NCTE). Secondary-school English teachers, other educators. Annual convention, publications, mailing lists, state affiliates.

1111 Kenyon Rd.
Urbana, IL 61801
800-369-6283
www.ncte.org

Children's Literature Association (ChLA). Academics studying the field of children's literature. Conferences, publications, foreign affiliates.

P.O. Box 138
Battle Creek, MI 49016
616-965-8180
chla@mlc.lib.mi.us
http://ebbs.english.vt.edu/chla/

Online Resources

World Wide Web

Aaron Shepard's Kidwriter Page. My own online resources for children's writers. Check here for updates and supplements to this book.

www.aaronshep.com/kidwriter

Author Online! My own home page. Among other things, you'll find Web versions of all my author promo pieces.

www.aaronshep.com

Children's Literature Web Guide. A wonderful guide to a wide variety of resources. Maintained by David K. Brown of the University of Calgary.

www.ucalgary.ca/~dkbrown

Inkspot. Resources and resource listings for all writers, with much for children's writers.

www.inkspot.com

The Purple Crayon. Articles, inside tips, and resource links from children's book editor Harold Underdown.

www.underdown.org

Raab Associates. Home page of a prominent children's book promotion agency. Includes numerous installments of Susan Raab's "To Market" column from the *SCBWI Bulletin.*

www.raabassociates.com/books.htm

eBook Connections. An excellent center of information on the field of electronic publishing.

www.ebookconnections.com

eBookNet. Another major site about electronic publishing.

www.ebooknet.com

MELVYL. The online catalog for the entire University of California library system. A sophisticated search function enables you to find resources in any subject area. If it's a serious book published within the last century anywhere, it's likely to be here. Once you have the bibliographic info, you can obtain a book locally through interlibrary loan.

www.melvyl.ucop.edu *or via*
www.cdlib.org

Eponym. Links to Web sites about personal names, including name lists from cultures around the world. Great for naming characters in multicultural stories.

www.eponym.org

Email Lists

Email lists are discussion groups by email. To subscribe to a list below, email the given subscription command to the given address. For example, for Letitia Comfort to subscribe to LM_NET, she would send just the one line "subscribe LM_NET Letitia Comfort" to listserv@listserv.syr.edu. The subject heading doesn't matter and can be left off.

Lists can bring you a lot of email! Most list software now gives you the option of receiving a digest—multiple messages sent in a single email—in place of individual messages. Look for the proper command in the instructions you get when you subscribe.

Note: Lists do NOT welcome messages with overt self-promotion.

CHILD_LIT. General discussion of children's literature. Subscribers include academics, teachers, public librarians, school librarians, and writers.

>subscribe CHILD_LIT *firstname lastname*
>listserv@email.rutgers.edu
>www.rci.rutgers.edu/~mjoseph/childlit/about.html

LM_NET. For school librarians. Has tight restrictions on messages seen as promoting a writer's work.

>subscribe LM_NET *firstname lastname*
>listserv@listserv.syr.edu
>http://ericir.syr.edu/lm_net/

PUBYAC. For public librarians.

>subscribe PUBYAC
>listproc@prairienet.org
>www.pallasinc.com/pubyac

Author Online!

For updates and more resources, visit
Aaron Shepard's Kidwriter Page at

www.aaronshep.com/kidwriter

Index

23830869R00068

Made in the USA
Lexington, KY
25 June 2013